PRAYER

All Prayer Makes All Things Possible

ASSESSMENT-ANSWER BOOK
(Answers to Multiple-choice and True/False Questions)

CHARLES MWEWA

Dedication

To Pastor Jim (*Ba Ngimu*)

&

Elder Kabulaya

Contents

Author's Word

This book is a companion text to the main text (ISBN: 978-1-988251-11-0) and it contains multiple-choice questions with answers, true/false questions with answers, essay-type questions without answers, the book's bibliography, the verses of Scripture cited and the abbreviations used in the main text. This book begins at Chapter 2, because Chapter 1 is the introduction in the main text. It is suggested that the student or reader must attempt the essay-type questions on their own or with the aid of their teachers using the materials provided in the main text. It is further advisable that students and readers must first make an attempt at answering the multiple-choice and true/false questions before referring to this answer book for confirmation.

cm.

Abbreviations Used in the Main Text

A.D	Anno Domini
ADS	Applied Digital Solutions
AIDS	Acquired Immune Deficiency Syndrome
AMP	Amplified Bible
B&L	Binding and Loosening
B.C	Before Christ
BLCI	Bread of Life Church International
CMS	Close-Mindedness Syndrome
Covid-19	Coronavirus Disease of 2019
EMCEE	Master of Ceremonies
ESV	English Standard Version
GPM	Gospel Promotion Ministries
HIV	Human Immunodeficiency Virus
ISA	Independent Spiritual Advice
KJV	King James Version
MMP	Mountain Moving Prayers
N.T.	New Testament
NASB	New American Standard Bible
NASV	New American Standard Version
NCV	New Century Version
NIV	New International Version
NKJV	New King James Version
O.T.	Old Testament
PAR	Principle of Active Receptivity
PIN	Personal Identification Number
U.S.	United States [of America]
WIBI	World Impact Bible Institute
WIV	World Influence Vision
ZWIPP	Zero-Worry Infinite Praying Principle

2 | Prayer Surveys from the Old Testament

Multiple-choice Questions

1. What is Colloquy?

   A. Tete-a-tete
   B. Face to face talk with God
   C. Asservation
   D. Appeal to the divine

2. The prayers contained in the Book of Psalms are both ___

   A. National and international prayers
   B. National and personal prayers
   C. Intimate and social prayers
   D. Davidic and Asaffic prayers

3. ___ is also known as the Book of Prayers.

   A. Proverbs
   B. Psalms
   C. Ecclesiastes
   D. Nehemiah

4. The ___ is the House of Prayer.

   A. Tabernacle
   B. Temple
   C. Human body
   D. Synagogue

5. During the "Moses to Judges" period, prayer was ___

   A. Appeal and intercession
   B. Appeal and prophetic blessing
   C. Colloquy and prophetic blessing
   D. Colloquy and intercession

True/False Questions

1. The temple is the house of prayer but the tabernacle is a place of sacrifices during the "Kingdom" period   **T**/F

2. During the "Psalms, Proverbs and Job" period, prayer is variously experienced by the supplicants.   **T**/F

3. Solomon's prayers were first for wisdom during the "Prophets" period. T/**F**

4. Hezekiah prays in national crises and for healing during his illness.   **T**/F

5. The Torah or the five books of law includes Genesis, Exodus, Leviticus, Judges and Deuteronomy.   T/**F**

6. Daniel proclaimed a fast at Ahava Canal.   T/**F**

7. In the Bible, enlightenment and quickening prayers are wildly repeated.   **T**/F

8. Most of David's psalms are praises.   T/**F**

9. Prophets are quintessentially intercessors.   **T**/F

10. The "Patriarchal" period is the duration of the three matriarchs or fathers.   T/**F**

Essay-type Questions

1. Define colloquy, and provide examples of biblical characters who engaged in such prayers

   [500 words or less].

2. Differentiate between "Book of Prayer" and "House of Prayer." How does one impact on the other?

   [250 words or less].

3. With scriptural proof, in which period, in your opinion, do we see a freer or a more grace-like approach to prayer?

   [250 words or less].

3 | Concepts of Prayer

Multiple-choice Questions

1. To most people, prayer is all about ____

    A. Asking
    B. Receiving
    C. Intercession
    D. Praise

2. All these constitute an intrinsic part of the concept of prayer, except ____

    A. Communication
    B. Commandment
    C. Order
    D. Relationship

3. All these may constitute communication media forms, except ____

    A. Verbal
    B. Applied
    C. Non-verbal
    D. Implied

4. Any of these may constitute types of forms of communication, except ____

   A. Digital
   B. Letters
   C. Public speaking
   D. Shouting

5. Any of these may constitute forms of new media, except ____

   A. Interactive media
   B. Zoom
   C. Social media
   D. TikTok

6. What is indispensable to communication?

   A. Feedback
   B. Medium
   C. Receiving
   D. Sending

Questions 7 is based on this verse of Scripture: "Ask and it will be given to you; seek and you will find; knock and the door will be opened to you" (Matt. 7:7).

7. What does the words – ask, seek, and knock – conceptualize in prayer?

   A. Communication
   B. Commission
   C. Commandment
   D. Relationship

8. What does the words "call," "answer," and "tell," illustrate in this verse of Scripture: "Call to me and I will answer you and tell you great and unsearchable things you do not know" (Jeremiah 33:3).

   A. Relationship
   B. Feedback
   C. Commandment
   D. Communication

9. The Mosaic Ten Commandments may also be called ____

   A. The Decameter
   B. The Decalogue
   C. Colloquy
   D. Collogue

10. Our personal prayer relationship with God is
___

A. Intimate
B. Casual
C. Contractual
D. Judicial

True/False Questions

1. A relationship is a loving association between two people. **T**/F

2. Relationships are backed by invisible rules which need to be observed. **T**/F

3. Relationships are anchored in intimacy. **T**/F

4. Prayer must be pale, dull and empty. T/**F**

5. Devotion is an aspect of intimacy. **T**/F

6. Both God and humans see the future. T/**F**

7. We must not trust that God hears and answers prayer. T/**F**

8. God does not have our best interest at heart. T/**F**

9. God is biased towards those who give money and they are the only ones He hears and answers when they pray. T/**F**

10. God may choose to answer prayer or not. **T**/F

Essay-type Questions

1. "Do not be anxious about anything, but in everything, by prayer and petition, with thanksgiving, present your requests to God. And the peace of God, which transcends all understanding, will guard your hearts and your minds in Christ Jesus" (Philippians 4:6-7). In relation to this passage, discuss the conception that the medium is the message.

   [250 words or less].

2. List and discuss the three basic concepts of prayer. [500 words or less].

4 | Defining Prayer

Multiple-choice Questions

1. The definition of prayer as talking to God is
___

   A. Anthropocentric
   B. Theocentric
   C. One-sided
   D. Homocentric

2. The definition of prayer as hearing from God
is ___

   A. Anthropocentric
   B. Theocentric
   C. One-sided
   D. Homocentric

Answer questions 3 to 5 using the following prayer below:

Prayer: "Dear heavenly Father, we thank you for this food which you have provided. Together with other benefits that you have bestowed upon us, we ask you to make this food worthy of our health and our praise of you. We believe that you have granted. In Jesus' name, Amen!"

3. A relationship is established by ___

    A. Reference to heavenly Father
    B. Reference to food
    C. reference to health
    D. Reference to praise

4. A communicative angle is established by ___

    A. Reference to heavenly Father
    B. Reference to food
    C. Reference to health
    D. None of the above

5. The phrase, "We believe that you have granted," establishes ___

    A. A relational trajectory
    B. Feedback
    C. A commandment trajectory
    D. Faith

True/False Questions

1. A soliloquise self-talk is the best definition of prayer.   T/**F**

2. Prayer is a regular dialogue between God the Father and His children for different reasons through the name of Jesus Christ.   **T**/F

3. Prayer must be based on a relationship between Father God and His children.
    T/F

4. The way one defines prayer may also be the way one prays. **T**/F

5. Defining prayer well does not affect one's prayer life. T/**F**

Essay-type Questions

1. Prayer is a regular dialogue between God the Father and His children for different reasons through the name of Jesus Christ.

    a) In this definition, locate the communication component.
    b) In this definition, locate the relationship component.
    c) In this definition, locate the commandment component.

    [500 words or less].

5 | Aspects of Prayer

Multiple-choice Questions

1. Looking at prayer from different perspectives constitutes ____

    A. Aspects of prayer
    B. Concept of prayer
    C. Types of prayer
    D. None of the above

2. All these have an aspect of request to them, except ____

    A. Supplication
    B. Petition
    C. Asking
    D. Praise

3. A suppliant seeks for ____

    A. Mercedes benz
    B. Ticket to a soccer match
    C. Food to eat
    D. A new attire to impress friends

4. A petitioner may seek for all these, except ___

   A. Mercedes benz
   B. Ticket to a soccer match
   C. Food to eat
   D. A new attire to impress friends

5. "Hannah was in deep anguish, crying bitterly as she prayed to the Lord. And she made this vow: 'O Lord of Heaven's Armies, if you will look upon my sorrow and answer my prayer and give me a son, then I will give him back to you. He will be yours for his entire lifetime, and as a sign that he has been dedicated to the Lord, his hair will never be cut'" (1 Samuel 1:10-11). What aspect of prayer does Hannah pray in this passage?

   A. Petition
   B. Prayers
   C. Intercession
   D. Thanksgiving

True/False Questions

1. Intercession is standing in the gap.   **T**/F

2. An intercessor is a watchman who alerts others about impending trouble or danger.
    T/F

3. Promptings are impressions or convictions that alight upon one's conscience.
    T/F

4. Thanksgiving can be the end in itself.
    T/F

5. Jesus prayed a prayer of thanksgiving.
    T/F

6. Thanksgiving cannot be a sacrifice.
    T/**F**

7. We should only thank God when something good happens to us, not when something bad happens.   T/**F**

8. Thanksgiving ensures permanence and continuity.   **T**/F

9. When we thank God, or even our fellow men, we are indicating that we are ready for more blessings.   **T**/F

10. Lack of thanksgiving is godly.   T/**F**

Essay-type Questions

1. Conceptualize the Philippians 4:6-7 Principle. Why is turning worry into a request important?

   [500 words or less].

6 | Types of Prayer

Multiple-choice Questions

1. There are two types of prayer, and these are
   _____ and ___

   A. Voiced; meditative
   B. Meditative; supplication
   C. Petition; voiced
   D. Meditative; requests

2. Any of these could constitute voiced prayer,
   except ___

   A. Adoration
   B. Praise and worship
   C. Requests
   D. Compositio loci

3. One of the disadvantage of voiced prayer is
   that ___

   A. It doesn't get answered
   B. God overlooks it
   C. Pride and ambition can muffle it's
   outcome
   D. One can't distinguish between genuine
   thoughts and the utterance

4. What test must both voiced and meditative prayers meet?

   A. Faith
   B. Confidence
   C. Love
   D. Intimacy

5. The Greek word Sumballo may mean all these, except ____

   A. To throw together
   B. To scatter
   C. To confer
   D. To ponder

True/False Questions

1. Colloque and colloquy both mean the same thing in prayer.   T/**F**

2. The resolve, which is the pouring out of devotion to God, happens only during colloquy.   T/**F**

3. The goal of meditation is the glory of God and to enlighten the human soul.
   T/F

4. At the petition stage, we begin to make our case known to God through our imagination.
   T/F

5. The meditation stage is that time in Meditative Prayer when we concentrate our minds on God.   T/**F**

6. The confession of sins and preparing of the heart to meet God happens at colloque.
   T/**F**

7. Men look at the heart but God looks at the outward appearance.   T/**F**

8. Meditative prayer engages thoughts.
   T/F

9. Most of the prayers one can make in their lifetime happens in the thoughts.
   T/F

10. All forms of yoga is evil.   T/**F**

Essay-type Questions

1. List and describe the five stages of meditation.

    [500 words or less].

2. "Let the words of my mouth and the meditation of my heart be acceptable in Your sight, O Lord, my rock and my Redeemer" (Psalm 19:14).

    a) How many types of prayer do you recognize in this assertion?
    b) Why is it important to train our minds and hearts into meditative prayer?

    [250 words or less].

7 | Deictics of Prayer

Multiple-choice Questions

1. The deictic of prayer relate to all these, except
    ___

    A. Place
    B. Subject
    C. Time
    D. Posture

2. The other name for posture is ___

    A. Manner
    B. Type
    C. Prostrate
    D. Pause

3. In which of these places have people prayed?

    A. Under water and at shores
    B. In the house and on mountains
    C. In prison
    D. All of the above

4. Hannah played ____

    A. Near the temple
    B. Near the tabernacle
    C. On top of Mount Sinai
    D. Inside a fish belly

5. Where does Jesus Christ discourages people to pray from or at?

    A. Synagogues
    B. Temples
    C. Street corners
    D. In the bedroom

6. In the early Church, they regularly prayed at this time, except ____

    A. 9 am
    B. 12 pm
    C. 3 pm
    D. 7 pm

7. How many times per day did Daniel pray in his house?

    A. 3
    B. 23
    C. 13
    D. 2

8. At what time was Cornelius fasting?

   A. 4 pm
   B. 3 pm
   C. 1 pm
   D. 12 am

9. When does the Bible say that the voice of prayer is beautiful?

   A. In the morning
   B. In the afternoon
   C. In the evening
   D. At night

10. The most admired quality of anyone waiting upon God in prayer is ___

    A. Love
    B. Patience
    C. Courage
    D. Faith

True/False Questions

1. Posture is always vital to prayer.　　T/**F**

2. Posture may not include standing.　　T/**F**

3. The early Christians always stood up when they prayed.　T/**F**

4. The standard posture for prayer is kneeling.　**T**/F

5. Placing the face between the knees is also part of lying prostrate.　　**T**/F

6. Lifting up extended hands in prayer symbolizes the faith to receive from God.　**T**/F

7. The early Church usually stood up in prayer on Sundays.　　　**T**/F

8. Falling prostrate to the ground is a sign of weakness among Jewish believers.　T/**F**

9. Like a true Father He is, God must rejoice to hear our voices early in the morning.　**T**/F

10. God hears meditative prayers loud and clear.　**T**/F

Essay-type Questions

1. "'Our ancestors worshiped on this mountain, but you Jews claim that the place where we must worship is in Jerusalem.' 'Woman,' Jesus replied, 'believe me, a time is coming when you will worship the Father neither on this mountain nor in Jerusalem. You Samaritans worship what you do not know; we worship what we do know, for salvation is from the Jews. Yet a time is coming and has now come when the true worshipers will worship the Father in the Spirit and in truth, for they are the kind of worshipers the Father seeks. God is spirit, and his worshipers must worship in the Spirit and in truth'" (John 4:20-24).

    a) What is assumed in this passage in relation to deictics of prayer?
    b) What is ironic in this passage about the place of prayer?
    c) What does this passage imply about time and posture of prayer, if any?

    [500 words or less].

2. "The 24 elders bow down and worship in front of the one who sits on the throne, the one who lives forever and ever. They throw their victor's crowns in front of the throne and say, 'You are worthy, our Lord and God, to receive glory, honor, and power, because

you created all things; they came into existence and were created because of your will,'" (Revelation 4:10-11).

a) Discuss posture in prayer in relation to the above passage.

[500 words or less].

8 | Effective Prayer

Multiple-choice Questions

1. Stated factly, the two-prong test for the effectiveness of prayer is ____

   A. Prayer must be heard and answered
   B. Prayer must be heard and deferred
   C. Prayer must be answered and venerated
   D. Prayer must be heard and announced

2. Any of these may be the qualities of prayer, except ____

   A. Righteousness
   B. Faith
   C. The will of God
   D. The joy of prayer

3. Christians are already ____

   A. Righteous
   B. Holy
   C. Blessed
   D. All of the above

4. The process of being declared righteous is termed ___

   A. Justification
   B. Sanctification
   C. Glorification
   D. Hubris

5. What gave Abraham's descendants the knowledge of sin?

   A. Grace
   B. Mercy
   C. The Mosaic law
   D. The New Testament Covenant

True/False Questions

1. Justification towards righteousness is available to all nations.   **T**/F

2. God treats us according to His Son's obedience, and not our own obedience.
   T/F

3. God accepts sinners on the grounds of Christ's obedience and death.   **T**/F

4. Redemption is the action of regaining or gaining possession of the believer's soul in exchange for payment.   **T**/F

5. Righteousness has been imputed or credited to believers in Christ. **T**/F

6. When believers confess their sins to each other and pray for each other, they get healed. **T**/F

7. Righteousness is fulfilled in Christ, giving every believer the power to have their prayers heard by God. **T**/F

8. Prayer and faith are like twins. **T**/F

9. Faith makes Christians believe that God answers prayer. **T**/F

10. Prayer is both the medium and the message of faith. **T**/F

Essay-type Questions

1. List and explain the five qualities of an effective prayer.

   [1,500 words or less].

9 | Ways through which God Speaks

Multiple-choice Questions

11. Jehovah-Shammah means ___

    E. God is there
    F. God shall provide
    G. God is our righteousness
    H. God is all-knowing

12. The conception that God spoke in the past, that He is speaking in the present, and that He will continue to speak in future is termed ___

    A. The Hebraic Gist
    B. The Speaking God
    C. The Gist
    D. The Hebraic

13. Who chooses the media to speak through?

    A. God
    B. People
    C. Pastors
    D. Parents

14. The two methods of speech God may use to speak to people are ___

    A. Directly or indirectly
    B. Directly or by word of mouth
    C. Indirectly or by using angels
    D. Implied and explicitly

15. To be able to learn how God speaks, one must do all these, except ___

    A. Cultivate a rich prayer habit
    B. Be open
    C. Know God's nature
    D. Attend many churches

True/False Questions

1. The God who spoke in the Bible and the one who speaks to us directly are different.
    T/**F**

2. God sometimes defiles His own Word.
    T/**F**

3. Satan is pretty much reliable.   T/**F**

4. God's voice is gentle.   **T**/F

5. CMS stands for close-mindedness syndrome.
    T/F

6. Close-mindedness and clear-mindedness may mean the same thing.   T/**F**

16. In obeying God's voice, feelings and emotions can be a blessing.   T/**F**

17. The attribute of omnipotence, means that God has absolute power.   **T**/F

18. The existence of God within tiny and minute formations is referred to as transcendence.   T/**F**

19. Worship is not a form pf prayer.   T/**F**

20. God can speak through inspired dreams, but only if He wants to punish someone.   T/**F**

Essay-type Questions

"Benjie is a young Christian who has been having challenges hearing from God. You have been a student of prayer where you learned about ways through which God speaks. Benjie strongly believes that the voices he is hearing in his head are confusing. He is not sure whether he is listening to God, the devil or from his own mind. Besides, when he was praying this morning, he saw something very clearly. It was a storm of rain which ended abruptly. He is not sure whether he was dreaming or he was in a trance when he saw it. It had happened very fast. Just before he left his home this morning, he was holding his Bible when it fell off his hand and automatically opened at Psalm 107:29, which read, 'He stilled the storm to a whisper; the waves of the sea were hushed.' He thinks that the storm he saw has something to do with this verse. Now he is completely confused and he comes to you for answers."

1. Explain to Benjie about the Hebraic Gist.
2. Explain to Benjie the direct and indirect methods God uses to speak to people.
3. How can Benjie be sure that the voices he is hearing are from God?
4. Explain to Benjie how he can distinguish a dream from a vision (trance).
5. You believe strongly that Benjie needs to know how to hear when God speaks directly. What advice can you give him?

[1,500 words or less].

10 | Legality of Prayer

Multiple-choice Questions

1. Even though prayer is a grace, it is also a _____

   I. Right
   J. Privilege
   K. Promise
   L. All of the above

2. Believers in Christ can lay claim to the promises of God on account of ____

   A. Death of Christ
   B. Resurrection of Christ
   C. Death and resurrection of Christ
   D. All of the above

3. The Grace Formula may be explicated as ____

   A. Right + Power + Command
   B. Right + Power
   C. Right + Command
   D. Command + Power

4. As a grace, prayer can be compared to all these, except ____

   A. A parent who both prepares a delicious meal for her child and commands her to eat it.
   B. A doctor who combines a healing concoction for a very sick patient and commands him to take it.
   C. A police officer who orders a motorist to disembark from his car
   D. A pastor who spend an hour preparing a sermons and delivers it to his congregation in thirty minutes.

5. How many promises are in the Bible?

   A. 5000
   B. 7,147
   C. 8,899
   D. 5487

6. Praying without ceasing may mean all these, except ____

   A. Without stopping
   B. Continually
   C. At all times
   D. Sometimes

7. The fact that God deals with us both legally and graciously entail ____

   A. That His relationship with people cannot be broken by Him
   B. Permanency
   C. Consistency
   D. All of the above

8. All these were implied in the Old Covenant, except ____

   A. Noahic Covenant
   B. Abrahamic Covenant
   C. Mosaic Covenant
   D. New Covenant

9. The Davidic Covenant was also known as ____

   A. Royal Covenant
   B. Covenant of Redemption
   C. Covenant of Grace
   D. Covenant of Works

10. All these may mean the same thing, except ____

   A. Mediator
   B. Internunciator
   C. Reconciler
   D. Adjudicator

True/False Questions

1. A testament is a will left by a person with instructions of their wishes of how their estate is to be distributed to beneficiaries after their death. **T**/F

2. A permanent agreement must be covenanted through blood. **T**/F

3. There is no need for a mediator unless there is more than one party involved in a dispute. **T**/F

4. Believers' inheritance is guaranteed. **T**/F

5. A will is unenforceable unless the testator dies. **T**/F

6. In English law, one cannot be both a mediator and a witness in the same matter. **T**/F

7. Adoption is both an act of grace and of love. **T**/F

8. Redemption necessitates reconciliation and adoption. **T**/F

9. Redemption is a legal act while reconciliation is a political or social act. **T**/F

10. A judge must be objectively open-minded, fair, independent, and decisive.   **T**/F

Essay-type Questions

1. Discuss the advocacy of Christ in relation to prayer. Use Scripture reference.

    [500 words or less]

2. List and discuss the four characteristics that every judge must possess. Relate these to God as a Judge.

    [250 words or less].

3. "Mercy has no value without wrath." Discuss.

    [250 words or less].

4. Discuss the concept of family by reference to adoption and inheritance bequeathed to believers in Christ Jesus.

    [500 words or less].

5. "Truly, truly, I tell you, whoever believes in Me will also do the works that I am doing. He will do even greater things than these because I am going to the Father. And I will do whatever you ask in My name, so that the

Father may be glorified in the Son. If you ask Me for anything in My name, I will do it," (John 14:12-14).

Discuss a believer's right in view of this passage of Scripture. [250 words or less].

11| Receiving under Law and Grace

Multiple-choice Questions

11. The word "conditional" is synonymous with ___

    M. Grace
    N. Law
    O. Moses
    P. Chapter 33 Promises

12. The word "unconditional" is synonymous with ___

    Q. Grace
    R. Law
    S. Moses
    T. Chapter 33 Promises

Questions 3 to 5 are based on the following prayer:

Isaiah prayed: "O LORD, be gracious to us! We wait for You. Be our strength every morning and our salvation in time of trouble," (Isaiah 33:2)

13. This prayer was one of seeking after ____

   A. Grace
   B. Fortitude
   C. Protection
   D. All of the above

14. What is implied in this prayer?

   A. Fortitude
   B. Patience
   C. Grace
   D. Protection

15. All these are requisitioned in this prayer, except ____

   A. Fortitude
   B. Patience
   C. Grace
   D. Protection

True/False Questions

1. Isaiah foretold the grace dispensation.
   T/F

2. Under Grace, prayer was conditional.
   T/**F**

3. Under Law, prayer was invitational.
    T/**F**

4. Chapter 33 Promises are of grace.
    T/F

5. Chapter 29 Promises are of law.
    T/F

6. Chapter 33 Promises have been fulfilled
    through Jesus Christ.   **T**/F

7. Believers in Christ are invited to pray and to
    legally receive all the blessings available to
    them in the spiritual places.   T/**F**

8. Jesus Christ was born under law.
    T/**F**

9. Jesus Christ was born of a woman.
    T/F

10. There was a partial fulfilment of grace before
    the fulness of time came.   **T**/F

Essay-type Questions

1. List and discuss the five factors of prayer and
    receiving.

    [500 words or less].

45

2. Define Chapter 33 promises.

   [250 words or less].

3. Define Chapter 29 promises.

   [250 words or less].

12 | Principles of Receiving

Multiple-choice Questions

16. Each of these is true, except ___

    U. God does answer prayer
    V. God does hear prayer
    W. Receiving from God is a science
    X. Receiving from God is art

17. PAR stands for ___

    A. Principle of Active Receptivity
    B. Please Act Receptively
    C. Principle of Actions and Receiving
    D. Power of Active Receptivity

18. Believing that God will provide and ending there is called ___

    A. Active receptivity
    B. Passive receptivity
    C. Active engagement
    D. Passive engagement

19. Under PAR, the question become ____

    A. Does God answer prayer?
    B. Does God listen to prayer?
    C. Do we know how to appropriate our answered prayers?
    D. Do we know how to record our uttered prayers?

20. All these constitute the three laws of PAR, except ____

    A. Law of Importunity
    B. Law of Right Inward Attitude
    C. Law of Right Outward Posture
    D. Lambano Law

True/False Questions

1. Importunity is persistence. **T**/F

2. God is Spirit; to answer our prayer, He needs a medium. **T**/F

3. Receiving entails the application of wisdom, patience, knowledge and skill on your part. **T**/F

4. The blessing is not in knocking, but knocking at the right door. **T**/F

5. Knocking is action. **T**/F

6. Matthew 7:7 is a principle arriving from the Luke 11:5-8. **T**/F

7. Persistence is a norm rather than an exception in the art of receiving from God. **T**/F

8. Persistence is not lack of faith; it is the re-energization of faith. **T**/F

9. "Blessing" may mean prosperity, favor, wellbeing, welfare, or good health. **T**/F

10. Faith needs action to be complete. **T**/F

Essay-type Questions

1. "Then Elisha said, 'Take the arrows!' So he took them, and Elisha said to the king of Israel, 'Strike the ground!' So he struck the ground three times and stopped. But the man of God was angry with him and said, 'You should have struck the ground five or six times. Then you would have struck down Aram until you had put an end to it. But now you will strike down Aram only three times.' 20And Elisha died and was buried," (2 Kings 13:18-20).

Exemplify the Law of Importunity using the above passage of Scripture.

[500 words or less].

2. Why is Jeremiah 33:3 sometimes known as "God's phone number"?

[250 words or less].

3. Exemplify the Law of Importunity using Jacob's encounter with God in genesis 32:22-29.

[500 words or less].

4. Define prayer attendance.

[250 words or less].

5. Define the PAR principle. How does using the PAR principle help believers to be actively involved in receiving from God?

[500 words or less].

13 | Salvation Plan

Multiple-choice Questions

1. The cross is a symbol of all these, except ____

   A. Unity
   B. Suffering
   C. Redemption
   D. Pleasure

2. Which statement illustrates the Principle of Divine Victory?

   A. A husband who takes an adulterous wife on an expensive vacation.
   B. A student who receives an A+ even when he missed three quarters of the semester.
   C. A pastor who is blessed with a bonus for having preached seventy sermons in a year.
   D. A child who is rewarded for bulling another child at camp.

3. The Kingdom of Darkness wins sometimes because ___

   A. It dominates everybody
   B. Satan is very powerful
   C. It finds it easier to be rewarded with bad for bad
   D. It finds it easier to be rewarded with good for good

4. The Divine Law of Justice was fulfilled ___

   A. In Christ's death
   B. In Christ's resurrection
   C. In Christ's ascension
   D. When Satan imprisoned Christ in hell

5. Jesus Christ fulfilled the Law of Righteousness ___

   A. When He hang on a tree
   B. When H dined with His disciples
   C. When He rose again from the dead
   D. When He fed 5000 people

True/False Questions

1. The devil is the very opposite of God.
   T/F

2. Our fight is not a dirty fight, but a good fight of faith.   **T**/F

3. When man (Adam and Eve) sinned in the Garden of Eden, the divine law of justice applied.   **T**/F

4. By being obedient to the commandments of his God, man had everything to fear on earth.
   T/**F**

5. Satan still has victory over the human race.
   T/**F**

6. And according to the Law almost all things are purged with blood, and without shading of blood there is no remission.   **T**/F

7. Satan emerged the winner at Calvary.
   T/**F**

8. Jesus was the Seed of a woman.   **T**/F

9. The death of Jesus Christ was only possible because God permitted it.   **T**/F

10. The death and resurrection of Christ paved a way to acceptable prayer.   **T**/F

Essay-type Questions

1. Explain the Principle of Divine Victory using at least two verses of Scripture.

   [250 words or less].

2. Explain the Divine Law of Justice using at least two verses of Scripture.

   [250 words or less].

3. Explain the dilemma of the two trees using at least two verses of Scripture.

   [250 words or less].

4. Explain the concept of the Seed of a woman using at least two verses of Scripture.

   [250 words or less].

5. Explain the Law of Righteousness using at least two verses of Scripture.

   [250 words or less].

14 | The Cross of Christ

1. The t-shaped cross is also known as ___

   A. Dagger
   B. St. Andrews
   C. St. Anthony
   D. Romania

2. The x-shaped cross is also known as ___

   A. Dagger
   B. St. Andrews
   C. St. Anthony
   D. Romania

3. Jesus must have been crucified on a ___ cross.

   A. Dagger-shaped
   B. St. Andrews
   C. St. Anthony
   D. Romania

4. The cross was foolishness to the ___

    A. Romans
    B. Greeks
    C. Jews
    D. Gentiles

5. To believers, the cross is ___

    A. The power of God
    B. The representation of Christ's humility
    C. The wisdom of God
    D. All of the above

True/False Questions

1. Crucifixion was practiced in the Old Testament.   T/**F**

2. Stoning was never practiced in the Old Testament.   T/**F**

3. In Roman Empire, crucifixion was the highest form of punishment.   T/**F**

4. Phoenicians and Carthagians did not practiced crucifixion.   T/**F**

5. No-one knows what type of cross Christ Jesus was crucified on.   T/**F**

6. Jesus Christ died quickly on the cross because they broke his lefts.   T/**F**

7. The Romans treated a crucified criminal as a slave.   **T**/F

8. The cross brought Jews and Gentiles together.   **T**/F

9. The victim's legs were twisted so that the calves were parallel to the crossbeam to induce pain.   **T**/F

10. Christian disciples must carry their crosses daily and follow Christ.   **T**/F

Essay-type Questions

1. List and explain the 10 stages of crucifixion, using Scripture, where possible.

    [500 words or less].

2. Compare the Greeks, the Romans, the Jews and Gentiles in regard to each's view of crucifixion.

    [500 words or less].

3. Justify the statement, "The cross is the power of God," using Scripture.

    [500 words or less].

15 | Grace Concept of Agape Love

Multiple-choice Questions

1. What is the highest level of character in Christianity?

    A. Love
    B. Agape love
    C. Filial love
    D. Erotic love

2. Agape love is all these, except ____

    A. Highest love
    B. Hallmark of the Christian faith
    C. Cornerstone of Christian belief
    D. All of the above are correct

3. All these may constitute the three tenets of agape love, except ____

    A. It sacrifices
    B. It betrays
    C. It gives
    D. It protects

4. Agape love may display all these, except
   ___

   A. Kindness
   B. Selfishness
   C. Patience
   D. Humility

5. All these will be nothing without agape love, except

   A. Service
   B. Worship
   C. Prayer
   D. All of the above are nothing without love

True/False Questions

1. Christianity is a dead religion without love.
   T/F

2. Love must be the pre-eminent virtue in life.
   T/F

3. Without love, our actions are just like noise.
   T/F

4. Man is a vengeful animal.   **T**/F

5. Gossip and bickering show that there is no love.   **T**/F

6. Love and giving go hand in hand. **T**/F

7. You have never loved until you are able to give up something valuable for your beloved.
   T/F

8. Life is the highest sacrifice one can ever make.
   T/F

9. Agape love is not an excellence.
   T/**F**

10. Love values truth. **T**/F

Essay-type Questions

1. List and describe the four tenets of agape love.

   [1000 words or less].

16 | Concept of Freedom

Multiple-choice Questions

1. True prosperity is ___

   A. Material wealth
   B. Having status symbols
   C. Possession of valuables and luxuries
   D. None of the above

2. The prayer that is grace-based and freedom-inclined should include all of the following, except ___

   A. Acceptability in Christ
   B. Activated account
   C. Prosperity God's way
   D. Less and less of thanksgiving

3. What did the Jewish people inherit in Abraham?

   A. Faith and prosperity
   B. Lands and cars
   C. Dreams and visions
   D. Faith and boats

4. The most basic God gives us in prayer are all these, except ___

   A. Daily bread
   B. Good health
   C. Protection from evil
   D. **Vacations**

5. To watch and pray includes all these, except ___

   A. Being aware of what God is doing
   B. Being aware of what the devil is planning
   C. **Being worried and anxious**
   D. Being alert

True/False Questions

1. Truth trumps theology. **T**/F

Essay-type Questions

1. Discuss balanced prosperity. Why do we need this knowledge in view of the modern movements that tend to equate prosperity to excessive materialism?

    [500 words or less].

17 | Prayer as Activated Account

Multiple-choice Questions

1. The concept of activated account assumes that ____

    A. Prayer is heard the moment it is uttered
    B. Answers may depend on different levels of expectations
    C. Faith and the will of God has everything to do with answers to prayer
    D. All of the above are correct

2. Spiritual ____ is inevitable to activated prayer accounts.

    A. Goodness
    B. Battle
    C. Harangue
    D. Fruit

3. The exchange between Archangel Gabriel and Daniel illustrate ____

    A. That words matter
    B. That words uttered in prayer matter
    C. That words uttered in prayer to God matter
    D. All of the above are correct

4. What's Satan's greatest hindrance to prayer?

   A. Prayerlessness
   B. Pride
   C. Envy
   D. Slumber

5. What does the new terms of our engagement require patience in the transactions of prayer and responses?

   A. Love
   B. Patience
   C. Favor
   D. Peace

True/False Questions

1. Patience is required otherwise the benefits of his prayer may be lost. **T**/F

2. When we pray, God will know and hear us. **T**/F

3. Answering prayer is a new God-man vocabulary. **T**/F

4. God only hears our prayers but He does not answer them. T/**F**

5. God hears prayers, answers prayer and provides that for which we have requested.
T/F

6. Prayer unleashes God's powerful princes to fight our battles. **T**/F

7. When we pray, we are surrendering our battles to God. **T**/F

8. God can command Satan and devils to do His bidding on our behalf. **T**/F

9. When we pray in the authority of the name of Jesus Christ, no prince or power of darkness can stand up against God's authoritative command. **T**/F

10. It is our duty to pray, how God decides to answer us is His prerogative. **T**/F

Essay-type Questions

1. Discuss prayer as an opened account with scriptural references to back up your answers.[

    500 words or less].

2. Explain the apparent discrepancy: Why should believers in Christ engage in spiritual warfare if God does not need a third-party media to intervene in delivering prayer answers?

    [750 words or less].

18 | Introduction to Intercession

Multiple Choice Questions

1. Both entugchano and paga have one thing in common:

   A. Light upon
   B. Meet accidentally
   C. Meet by chance
   D. At any place

2. Which quality must define all intercessors?

   A. Prayerfulness
   B. Faithfulness
   C. Good character
   D. Holiness

3. Intercession is a _____ centered ministry.

   A. People
   B. God
   C. Holy Spirt
   D. Jesus

4. Who in the Old Testament exemplifies the intercessory concept?

   A. Jacob
   B. Moses
   C. Abraham
   D. Nehemiah

5. Intercession is an act of _____

   A. Grace
   B. Power
   C. Human will
   D. Personal effort

6. Intercessions are _____, which are done in a particular place and at a particular time for a particular person or persons for a particular purpose or results.

   A. Actions
   B. Dreams
   C. Promptings
   D. Words

True or False Questions

1. An Old Testament watchman was a kind of an intercessor. **T**/F

2. Intercessors must make themselves righteous. T/**F**

3. It is through prayer that people, communities and nations are brought before God. **T**/F

4. It isn't very vital to note, though, that our acquiescence to be led by the Holy Spirit is an act of grace on the part of God and not of our own wilful volition. T/**F**

5. No sooner we realize how important it is to know God personally than we begin to understand how good God is. **T**/F

6. A biblical intercessor always identifies with people using the "I" word vocabulary in prayer. T/**F**

7. The Decalogue is the only set of regulations God expected the Israelites to follow. T/**F**

Essay-type Questions

1. Review the concepts of Entugchano and Paga and ascertain how they illustrate the intercessory concept.

    [500 words or less].

2. Discuss five of the qualities of an intercessor.

    [500 words or less].

3. How does Jacob' encounter with God justify the modern Holy Spirit-breathed intercession?

    [500 words or less].

4. Identify at least two needs for intercessors and discuss why this is essential to the work of the Great Commission.

    [500 words or less]

19 | System of Intercession

Multiple Choice Questions

1. According to this chapter, which one of the following statements is true?

    A. Only intercessors must pray
    B. Intercession is only a gift
    C. As a gift, only pastors are intercessors
    D. Every Christian is commanded to pray

2. Each of this is a category of intercessors recognized in this chapter, except:

    A. General
    B. Crisis
    C. Warfare
    D. Intervention

3. A mark of true intercessors is that ___

    A. They pray longer
    B. They fast frequently
    C. They have a special gift
    D. They pray

4. All these are intercessors, except:

    A. Jesus Christ
    B. Holy Spirit
    C. Personal Intercessors
    D. God

5. Intercessors ____

    A. Must constantly advise the person they pray for
    B. Must always be found
    C. Must belong to an intercessory ministry
    D. Must be sensitive to the prompting of the Holy Spirit

True or False Questions

1. Intercession can be both a role and a gift in one individual.   **T**/F

2. Intercessors must hide the sin of the person they pray for from people but only disclose it before God. **T**/F

3. Jesus Christ is the intercessor of intercessors   T/**F**

4. Every Christian is commanded to pray.   **T**/F

5. Warfare intercessors do spiritual warfare on a more regular basis than any other category   **T**/F

Essay-type Questions

1. "Praying for longer hours does not signal superiority in intercessory mastery, just as praying relative shorter prayers does not indicate intercessory inferiority." Discuss this statement.

    [500 words or less].

2. List and describe at least five (5) qualities of personal intercessors.

    [300 words or less].

3. Explain intercession as a grace (refer to other chapters in this book).

    [500 or less words].

4. Explain the concept of "wrestling" with its derivatives in relation to Epaphras.

    [250 words or less]

5. Define spiritual martyrdom" and relate it to Satan's desire to destroy Personal Intercessors.

    [250 words or less].

20 | The Heart of Intercession

Multiple-choice Questions

1. The word paga conceptualizes all of these, except:

   A. Urgency
   B. Place
   C. **Power**
   D. Chance

2. Intercession may be synonymized by all these, except:

   A. Lawyer
   B. Advocate
   C. **Adjudicator**
   D. Mediator

3. Prayer may action all of the following, except:

   A. Salvation
   B. Forgiveness
   C. **Personal glory**
   D. Peace and eternal life

4. In the Old Testament, a ___ stood in the gap on behalf of the people.

   A. Medium
   B. King
   C. Priest
   D. Prophet

5. "As soon as God hears, He will answer you," illustrates:

   A. Grace
   B. Glory
   C. Conditional grace
   D. Unmerited glory

True/False Questions

1. Paga means an accidental meeting place; to come to a place by chance; and to discover that God is there.   **T**/F

2. An intercessor is someone who pleads the case of another.   **T**/F

3. Intercession is the power to reach out and take and establish what already belongs to us.   **T**/F

4. An intercessor is someone who takes hold of another's hand, on one hand, and that of the person being prayed for, on the other, and brings them together by standing in the gap.   T/**F**

5. God does not work with men.   T/**F**

6. The heart of an intercessor is to receive and to pray no matter what the cost.
    T/**F**

Essay-type Questions

1. Distinguish between intercession and sacrifice.

   [250 words or less].

2. Discuss, "Intercessors are capable of reversing God's mind," in reference to Ezekiel 22:30-31 and Malachi 3:6.

   [500 words or less].

3. Relate intercession to the heart of the Father.

   [250 words or less].

21 | Watchmanship

Multiple-choice Questions

1. Where does a believer's help come from?

   A. Hills
   B. The Lord
   C. Angels
   D. Police

2. An Old Testament watchman is the New Testament equivalent of ___

   A. An evangelist
   B. An intercessor
   C. An usher
   D. An apostle

3. According to the Bible, watchmen should constantly be ___

   A. Making peace
   B. Praying
   C. Arguing
   D. Guarding

4. What is the symbol of refuge?

   A. Prayer
   B. Watching and praying
   C. Watching
   D. Prayer and fasting

5. What activates God's protection?

   A. Angels
   B. Prayer
   C. Watching
   D. Watchmen

True/False Questions

1. The core of our defence is God Himself, not the means through which God protects us.   **T**/F

2. God primarily protects us through angels.   T/**F**

3. Intercessors should give God plenty of rest. T/**F**

4. Watchmen, generally, performed two roles.   **T**/F

5. The centerpiece of our refuge is the conceptualization of the Lord as our rock. **T**/F

Essay-type Questions

1. "A watchman performed two roles: He guarded the walls of ancient towns for the welfare of its citizens and he warned of impending trouble."

   Discuss the intercessory concept in relation to this statement.

   [500 words or less].

2. Discuss the following statement: "Watching only without praying is a fantasy; praying only without watching is a detriment."

   [250 words or less].

3. "The success of the watchman [is] dependent upon God's grace and guidance." Discuss.

   [250 words or less].

22 | Prayer and Groaning

Multiple-choice Questions

1. Each of these is an element of the prayer of groaning, except:

   A. **Blessings**
   B. Faith
   C. Patience
   D. Action

2. Our groanings are a mark of ___

   A. Hard labor
   B. Love
   C. Works
   D. Deeds

3. Groanings are begotten by ___

   A. Love
   B. Hope
   C. The Holy Spirit
   D. Jesus

4. Travailing is the action of acute intercession and may also be termed as ___

   A. Spiritual breakthrough
   B. Groaned pleading
   C. Fervent praying
   D. Desperate praying

5. Each of these exemplifies the prayer of groaning, except:

   A. Lot
   B. Hannah
   C. Elijah
   D. Epaphras

True/False Questions

1. Our groanings are not a mark of hard labor, but rather, of the labor of love and grace.
   T/F

2. The Church has received such grace that it needs not be in labor to produce results, nor does she need to undergo the pain of labor. **T**/F

3. "Before she was in labor, she gave birth; before her pain came, she delivered a male child," is a statement of grace rather than of protest.   **T**/F

4. Because we can't make the right requests, the Holy Spirit who knows the will of God ensures that we get it right.   **T**/F

5. Groanings do not, under any circumstance, lead to deliverance from bandage.   T/**F**

Essay-type Questions

1. List and describe the four elements of the prayer of groaning.

    [250 words or less]

2. List and discuss the three facts of the Holy Spirit-begotten groanings.

    [250 words or less]

23 | Prayer and Praise

Multiple-choice Questions

1. Praise and worship are a form of ___

    A. Prayer
    B. Tradition
    C. Spiritual exercise
    D. Liturgy

2. Each of these mean the same thing in the context of God's presence, except:

    A. Suit
    B. Rule
    C. Dwell
    D. Inhabit

3. Glory cannot be defined without ___

    A. Praise
    B. Grace
    C. Power
    D. Love

4. The tabernacle is to sacrificial animals, the temple is to ___

   A. Prayer
   B. Praise
   C. Crops
   D. Altar

5. Praise and worship are a form of sacrifices under ___

   A. Grace
   B. Temple worship
   C. Law
   D. Tabernacle worship

True/False Questions

1. God inhabits the prayers of His people.
   T/**F**

2. Both praise and worship are a form of prayer. **T**/F

3. God can punish idolatry up to the fourth generation.   **T**/F

4. Only the Jews were created to worship God.   T/**F**

5. The primary purpose of a creature is to showcase the wisdom, creativity and resourcefulness of its creator. **T**/F

6. This chapter has identified a three-pronged rationale for the prayer of praise.   **T**/F

7. Through Jesus, we infrequently offer up a sacrifice of praise to God.   T/**F**

8. Under grace, the temple is at Jerusalem.
   T/**F**

9. Only part of the earth is full of the glory of God.   T/**F**

10. We grow closer to God by worship but not by fellowship. T/**F**

Essay-type Questions

1. "Humans are the only creatures capable of deliberate worship. They can subject their will to the worship of their Maker (God). If they choose otherwise, they will miss the exact purpose of their existence."

   Discuss.

   [250 words or less].

2. List and discuss the three-pronged rationale for the prayer of praise.

   [250 words or less].

3. "Praise is a double-edged sword; it cuts both ways. We enter into God's presence by means of praise, but we praise God because we are in His presence." Discuss.

   [250 words or less].

4. "Praise is the ultimate prayer." Discuss.

   [250 words or less].

24 | Prayer of Weeping

Multiple-choice Questions

1. The Which prophet is also known as the Weeping Prophet?

   A. Isaiah
   B. Hosea
   C. Joel
   D. Jeremiah

2. A warrior never accepts the presence, tactics or works of the ___

   A. Opponent
   B. Victim
   C. Enemy
   D. Victor

3. All these are principles of Weeping Prayer, except:

   A. Feeling God's heart
   B. Calling people to celebration
   C. A strong desire to see people's conditions change
   D. Breaking-up hard grounds

4. What is the shortest verse in the Bible?

   A. John 11:35
   B. 1 Thessalonians 5:16
   C. Eccl 3:4
   D. Esther 8:9

5. What is the longest verse in the Bible?

   A. John 11:35
   B. 1 Thessalonians 5:16
   C. Eccl 3:4
   D. Esther 8:9

True/False Questions

1. Like Jesus our Lord, we may weep, not because we are overcome with sadness, but because we desire to produce God's victory and joy. **T**/F

2. Roaring is a type of crying in which we make articulate sobbing sounds and call out aloud. T/**F**

3. Jesus was on earth to destroy the works of the enemy because God hates evil.
   T/F

4. Weeping brings out our champion in the Lord. T/**F**

5. Weeping in the Spirit is a form of sowing. **T**/F

6. The Holy Spirit-inspired weeping always produces joy. **T**/F

7. Satan has not been defeated but he will be defeated in future. T/**F**

8. God's roar shakes things. **T**/F

9. Jeremiah and Apostle Paul specifically referred to weeping as plowing the ground. T/**F**

10. Jesus is also called the Lion of the Tribe of Judah. **T**/F

Essay-type Questions

1. With reference to at least five (5) scriptures, explain how weeping brings out champions for the Lord.

   [500 words or less].

2. In reference to Jesus' name as the Lion of the Tribes of Judah, explain the significance of roaring. Refer to at least two (2) scriptures.

[250 words or less].

3. List and describe the six principles of a Weeping Prayer.

   [500 words or less].

4. "Paul uses words like 'sorrow,' 'sadness' and 'concern.' That is what a person burdened by the desire to change other people's conditions does or goes through." Discuss.

   [500 words or less].

25 | Prayer of Agreement

Multiple-choice Questions

1. _____ is central to both human and divine affairs.

   A. Unity
   B. Agreement
   C. Covenant
   D. Harmony

2. Any of these may qualify to be defined as an agreement, except:

   A. Walking together
   B. Similar mind
   C. Covenant
   D. Same judgment

3. According to the Multiplied Power of Prayer or MPP, one can chase a thousand, and two ___ to flight?

   A. Ten thousand
   B. Two thousand
   C. None
   D. A thousand and two

4. If a Church of 200 intercessors agree to pray on a request. How much result in multiplying power do they stand to gain in total?

    A. 2,000,000
    B. 200,000
    C. 200,000,000
    D. 2000

5. What is the key most ingredient in the Prayer of Agreement?

    A. It must be prayed by two or more people
    B. The people must be alive and on earth
    C. Asking the Father for something in the name of our Lord Jesus Christ
    D. There must be an agreement

True/False Questions

1. The Prayer of Agreement must be prayed by two or more people.   **T**/F

2. The Prayer of Agreement must be alive and on earth.   T/**F**

3. In the Prayer of Agreement, the two or more people alive on earth must ask the Father for something in the name of our Lord Jesus Christ.   **T**/F

4. The Prayer of Agreement must be in agreement.   **T**/F

5. In the Prayer of Agreement, agreement must be in truth and in spirit. **T**/F

6. The Prayer of Agreement should be a Mental Assent.   T/**F**

7. The two or more people in the Prayer of Agreement must ask together; it is not a casual prayer. **T**/F

8. When two or more people ask in the name of Jesus, the Lord will be there with them.   T/**F**

9. When praying a Prayer of Agreement, two or more people involved must forgive each other and their brethren.   **T**/F

10. The Prayer of Agreement involves binding and restricting. T/**F**

Essay-type Questions

1. Discuss the multiplied effect of the Prayer of Agreement.

   [500 words or less].

2. Define the Prayer of Agreement with respect to derivatives for agreement and the espoused ingredients.

   [500 words or less].

3. "With one accord they all continued in prayer, along with the women and Mary the mother of Jesus, and with His brothers " (Acts 1:14).

   Explain the significance of this verse in relation to the Prayer of Agreement.

   [500 words or less].

4. "Prayer made this way, does not only move the heavens, but it also moves the heart and soul."

   Cite a scriptural reference and explain the significance of this kind of prayer.

   [250 words or less].

26 | Prayer of Power

Multiple-choice Questions

1. Each of these may be an attribute of asking, except:

    A. We should say exactly what we need to say
    B. We should say exactly what we want to say;
    C. We should keep it simple, the fewer words the better
    D. It should be difficult to ask for requests

2. One of the reasons why people may not receive from God is because ___

    A. They have faith
    B. They have knowledge
    C. They don't give thanks
    D. They don't ask

3. Each of these prayed powerful weeping prayers, except:

    A. Jeremiah
    B. Hannah
    C. Jesus Christ
    D. Jonah

4. Jesus' power to work miracles was generated by ___

   A. Preaching
   B. Teaching
   C. Him being God
   D. Prayer

5. Righteous heart of faith + Voice of prayer =

   A. Glory
   B. Grace
   C. Freedom
   D. Power

True/False Questions

1. For your Father knows exactly what you need even before you ask him.
   T/F

2. You do not receive because you do not have.   T/**F**

3. Gold there is, and rubies in abundance, but lips that speak knowledge are a rare jewel.
   T/F

4. Grace and power can be likened to a rancher who resides on a piece of land laden with gold ores.   T/**F**

5. God has given His most precious gift and there is nothing else He can fail to give us.   **T**/F

6. The price of prayer is yet to be paid through hard praying and fasting.   T/**F**

7. Nehemiah's quiet prayer was fervent.   **T**/F

8. Common-sense would expect that God would be in a still, small voice. T/**F**

9. Grace works by faith.   **T**/F

10. For prayer to have power, it should be able to accomplish the purpose for which it was made.   **T**/F

Essay-type Questions

1. List and briefly discuss the seven-prong attitude for asking.

   [150 words or less].

2. Discuss the three grace foundation of a powerful prayer.

   [500 words or less].

3. Discuss the idea of fervency by citing at least three scriptural references from the Bible.

   [500 words or less].

4. How does prayer generate power?

   [250 words or less].

27 | Prayer of Forgiveness

Multiple-choice Questions

1. The What does it mean by forgiveness being a zero-option proposition?

   A. There are many options
   B. It's the only option or there is no other option
   C. It's an option sometimes
   D. It's never an option

2. Whether we can remember the offences we have forgiven or not is ___

   A. A definition of forgiveness
   B. A test of forgiveness
   C. An implication of forgiveness
   D. A duty to forgive

3. We forgive because ___

   A. God demands it
   B. God first forgave
   C. God will be saddened if we don't
   D. God will forgive us even if we don't forgive

4. The peace that surpasses all understanding is ___

   A. The power of prayer
   B. A benefit of the Prayer of Forgiveness
   C. A utility principle
   D. A requirement for making a request

5. The Prayer of Forgiveness must be a ___

   A. Duty
   B. Lifestyle
   C. Drudge
   D. Directive

6. The ultimate essence of the Prayer of Forgiveness is ___

   A. Joy
   B. **Freedom**
   C. Peace
   D. Hope

True/False Questions

1. The Love forgives. **T**/F

2. Forgiveness is an act of love.
   T/F

3. The Prayer of Forgiveness and the Prayer of Faith are inversely related.
   T/**F**

4. Prayer is a sacrifice of our hearts.
   T/F

5. Grace is in that God forgave us even before we asked for His forgiveness.
   T/F

6. God sometimes remembers the sins He has forgiven.   T/**F**

7. By forgiveness being infinite, it means that it is limitless.   **T**/F

8. We need to feel the need to forgive.
   T/**F**

9. There is a right and a wrong time to forgive.   T/**F**

10. The power of the Prayer of Forgiveness deals with our hearts.
    T/F

Essay-type Questions

1. By reference to at least five (5) scriptural verses, discuss the inclusivity of forgiveness.

   [500 words or less].

2. Differentiate forgiveness from the Prayer of Forgiveness.

   [250 words or less].

3. List and describe the five (5) implications of pro-giving.

   [250 words or less].

4. Discuss the tripartite benefits of the Prayer of Forgiveness

   [250 words or less].

5. "We make those who sin against us a prayer request." Discuss.

   [250 words or less].

28 | Prayer of Repentance

Multiple-choice Questions

1. The principles of repentance encapsulate a two-prong process of ___

    A. Believing and confessing
    B. Believing and repenting
    C. Confessing and righteousness
    D. Confessing and salvation

2. Repentance is a ___

    A. Prayer
    B. Grace
    C. Process
    D. Going forward

3. Repentance is the ___ form of prayer.

    A. Basic
    B. Complex
    C. Difficult
    D. Rare

4. Why is the Prayer of Repentance also called the Grace of Goodness?

    A. Because God does not want anyone to perish
    B. Because repentance shows God's goodness
    C. Because repentance is a grace
    D. All of the above are correct

5. Repentance is ____

    A. A prayer
    B. A prayer that God has commanded
    C. A prayer that God has commanded every creature
    D. A prayer that God has commanded every creature to pray

True/False Questions

1. Every creature is commanded to repent.
   T/F

2. Repentance is a two-prong process, it involves the mind and the mouth.
   T/**F**

3. When true repentance comes, change happens in the inside of us.
   T/F

4. Repentance means to change, to turn around and to go in the opposite direction.
   T/F

5. Believing doesn't make one righteous.
   T/**F**

6. Believing in Jesus as Lord brings salvation.
   T/F

7. Believing is followed by confession, which is made with the mouth unto righteousness. T/**F**

Essay-type Questions

1. "Those who cannot confess due to various reasons, will still be saved as long as they believe in their hearts." Discuss.

   [500 words or less].

2. Resolve the discrepancy by using the relevant verses of Scripture: "God is patient with sinners but sinners may die in sin at any time."

   [250 words or less].

3. "God, I am a sinner. I acknowledge that Jesus Christ died for me and took away my sins. I ask for your forgiveness. Write my name in the Book of Life and give me a new life in Christ. Amen." Review this Sinner's Prayer in the light of Romans 10:9-10 and Ephesians 2:8.

   [500 words or less].

29 | Prayer of Peace

Multiple-choice Questions

1. In the formula:

    Zero-worry + Prayer (Requests) +
    Thanksgiving = Peace (Heart &
    Soul/Jesus Christ)

    The condition of the heart and mind in
    Christ is related to worry ____

    A. Indirectly
    B. Inversely
    C. Proportionately
    D. Directly

2. In the *Transference of Cares*, we may transfer
    each of these, except ____

    A. Worry
    A. Anxieties
    C. Cares
    D. **Praise**

3. The Christian life is tied to ___

A. Peace
A. **Prayer**
C. Power
D. People

4. What should every Christian pray for and seek?

A. Power
B. **Peace**
C. Joy
D. Money

5. The divine framework is deeply imbued in ___ and partly imbued in ___.

A. Jesus; Us
B. Us; Jesus
C. God; Jesus
D. Jesus; God

6. ZWIPP stands for ___

A. **Zero-Worry Infinite Praying Principle**
B. Zero-Work Infinite Principle
C. Zero-Worry Inferential Praying Principle
D. Zero-Worry Infinite Praising Principle

True/False Questions

1. Prayer is the pathway to both power and peace. **T**/F

2. The prayer for peace, is peace in itself. **T**/F

3. The condition of the heart and mind in Christ is inversely related to worry.
    T/F

4. The Prayer of Peace is hugely anchored in human efforts.   T/**F**

5. The more we worry, the more peace we will find.   T/**F**

6. St. Francis of Assisi's "Lord, make me an instrument of your peace" prayer is founded in the second leg of divine framework.   **T**/F

7. The verse, "God cares for you, so turn all your worries over to him," is also known as the *Transference of Cares*. **T**/F

8. According to James, general trouble may be tackled by simply praying.   **T**/F

9. Christians are called to peace. **T**/F

10. In Christianity, peace is a process, not the result.   T/**F**

Essay-type Questions

1. Define the Prayer of Peace.

   [500 words or less].

2. Write down the ZWIPP formula and explain its constituent elements.

   [500 words or less].

3. We pray for peace in relation to its divine framework. Explain the efficacy of this framework.

   [250 words or less].

4. Explain the five (5) implications of *Transference of Cares*.

   [250 words or less].

30 | Mountain Moving Prayers

Multiple-choice Questions

1. MMP stands for ___

   A. Mountain Making Prayer
   B. Mountain Mowing Prayer
   C. Mountain Moving Prayer
   D. Money Making Power

2. All these are principles of MMP, except ___

   A. When God appears, problems disappear
   B. When God is angry, strongholds under Him can tremble
   C. Difficult situations can become even more difficult
   D. Problems may change state or conditions at the presence of God

3. The MMP is a ____ prayer, and not a "receiving" prayer.

   A. "Moving"
   B. "Moving in"
   C. "Moving away"
   D. "Away"

4. All these constitute some of the characteristics of an MMP, except ____

   A. It is based on spoken words
   B. It is addressed directly to the challenge
   C. **It concerns binding and loosening**
   D. The mountain must be sent away or commanded to go to a specific place

5. Mountains are mentioned at least ____ times in the Bible.

   A. 250
   B. 5000
   C. **500**
   D. 2500

True/False Questions

1. Mountains must be identified, ordered to move, and directed to specific locations.
   T/F

2. There is only one interpretation on the symbolism of mountains.   T/**F**

3. Mountains remind us of God's glory, the trials we face, victories we obtain through Christ, or refuge from the enemy.   **T**/F

4. Our Lord Himself frequented mountains to pray.   **T**/F

5. Mountains are symbols of many of the ups and downs of life.   **T**/F

6. Mountain moving prayers are defined as prayers that declare the removal of a challenge in strict faith.T/**F**

7. MMPs are always vocalized.   T/**F**

8. MMPs must always be sent to the sea. T/**F**

9. B&L should be the first action under Church discipline.   T/**F**

10. MMPs must be made under the authority of the name of Jesus Christ.   **T**/F

Essay-type Questions

1. Explain the grace principle of MMPs.

    [250 words or less].

2. Differentiate between faith as small as a mustard seed and little faith.

    [500 words or less].

3. "Poverty in my life, be removed and be thrown into Hell, in Jesus' name. Thank you, heavenly Father, that poverty has been removed. Now, Father, I ask that you give me strength and ideas and opportunities to make money, in Jesus' name, Amen!" Review this prayer in view of MMP and "receiving" prayer.

   [500 words or less].

4. List at least two scriptural verses and explain how MMP may cause conditions to change or to be changed.

   [250 words or less].

31 | Principles of Fasting

Multiple-choice Questions

1. The requirement not to pose as if one is fasting during fasting is called ____

   A. The law of secrecy
   B. Absolute fast
   C. Importunity
   D. Dormancy

2. Each of these is part of the inevitability of biblical fasting, except ____

   A. Covenant-writing effect
   B. Attention-arresting effect
   C. Total-commitment effect
   D. Consumption effect

3. Under grace, fasting is accompanied by all these, except ____

   A. Beauty
   B. Decency
   C. Honor
   D. Sackcloth

4. All these constitute the precautionary measures in fasting, except ____

   A. Starving the spirit man
   B. No over-eating
   C. No miserable-looking
   D. Drink adequate amount of water

5. All these are principles of fasting, except ____

   A. Purpose
   B. Hospitality
   C. Inspiration
   D. Showmanship

6. What is the first hurdle one must overcome in beginning a fasting engagement?

   A. The urge to eat
   B. The class of fasting
   C. The length of fasting
   D. The degree of commitment

7. Satan first tempted man with it, and then also tempted our Lord with it. What is it?

   A. Glory
   B. Pride
   C. Food
   D. Money

True/False Questions

1. The Under the law, fasting was a weapon of humiliation with guarantees for breakthrough.   T/**F**

2. Under grace, God has guaranteed a reward to those who will fast according to Jesus' stipulations.   **T**/F

3. When one fasts and God answers their prayers, this is called the Attention-arresting Effect.   **T**/F

4. In biblical fasting, praying and reading the Bible don't go hand in hand.   T/**F**

5. The reward of fasting comes from God and not from men.   **T**/F

6. Christians fast for their seen God.   T/**F**

7. Fasting is abstaining from solid foods and water in order to concentrate on a divine cause by means of prayer and the Word of God.   **T**/F

8. Biblical fasting is pointless without a well-defined purpose.   **T**/F

9. The reference to "afflict yourself" in the Day of Atonement alludes to fasting.   **T**/F

10. Paul rarely fasted.   T/**F**

Essay-type Questions

1. The Discuss the food imperative with the aid of scriptural verse/s.

   [500 words or less].

2. Classify fasting and give examples when each may be required

   [250 words or less].

3. "Abstaining from sex is permissible for a period of time if you both agree to it, and if it's for the purposes of prayer and fasting - but only for such times. Then come back together again. Satan has an ingenious way of tempting us when we least expect it." Discuss.

   [500 words or less].

4. What makes the New Testament approach to fasting one of grace?

   [250 words or less].

5. Explain the five presumptions of fasting.
   [500 words or less].

6. With the use of relevant scriptural reference, explain the pleasure-pain (food) imperative and justify why Satan uses it to tempt people.

   [500 words or less].

32 | Benefits of Fasting

Multiple-choice Questions

1. Esther instructed Mordecai to "not eat or drink for three days, night or day, and I and my maidens will fast as you do." This class of fasting is ____

   A. Total fast
   B. Partial fast
   C. Semi-complete fast
   D. The Esther-Fast

2. Complete the sentence: "Howbeit, this kind goeth not out but by prayer and ____."

   A. Fasting
   B. Actions
   C. Feasting
   D. Worship

3. Who said these words: "Set apart for me Barnabas and Saul for the work to which I have called them"?

   A. The Holy Spirit
   B. Jesus Christ
   C. Church at Antioch
   D. The Jerusalem Council

4.   All these are benefits of fasting, except ___

   A. Rewarding
   B. The will of God
   C. Baptism
   D. Divine deliverance

5.   The flesh or the bodily man has a/an ___

   A. Sinful nature
   B. Bloody nature
   C. Weak nature
   D. Eternal nature

True/False Questions

1. This chapter has identified twenty benefits of fasting.   T/**F**

2. Fasting is for spiritual VIPs only.
   T/**F**

3. The Bible talks of getting understanding rather than choice rubies.   **T**/F

4. Barnabas, Niger, Lucius and Manaen were prophets and teachers at Antioch.   **T**/F

5. God's presence is the same as God's power.
   T/F

6. Favor, among other sources, comes from fasting. **T**/F

7. Jeremiah ate no pleasant food, no meat or wine came into his mouth, nor did he anoint himself at all, till three whole weeks were fulfilled.   T/**F**

8. Joy is the immediate outcome of fasting.
   T/F

9. The "Repairer of Broken Walls, Restorer of Streets with Dwellings" is Jesus.   T/**F**

10. Prophet Isaiah gave guidelines on a fasting that is acceptable by God.   **T**/F

Essay-type Questions

1. List and describe in great details at least ten benefits of fasting pursuant to Isaiah 58.

    [1500 words or less].

33 | Introduction to Spiritual Warfare

Multiple-choice Questions

1. In international law, war must be ___ to be legal.

   A. **Declared**
   B. Discussed
   C. Defined
   D. Debated

2. A specific event of combat as opposed to the general nature of declaration of conflict, is called ___.

   A. War
   B. **Battle**
   C. Armistice
   D. Demilitarization

3. Satan's tripartite mechanism of evil includes ___

   A. **Lies; false knowledge; and argumentative thoughts**
   B. Lies; weapons; and knowledge
   C. False knowledge; demons; and argumentative thoughts
   D. Argumentative thoughts; lofty ideas; and wrong thinking

4. All these are principles of spiritual warfare, except ____

   A. It's spiritual
   B. It's weapons are spiritual
   C. Spiritual weapons have divine power
   D. There are two levels of strongholds

5. The weapons of our warfare are ____

   A. Livelily
   B. Physical
   C. Spiritual
   D. Canal

True/False Questions

1. War has a universal connotation.
   T/F

2. Battle is always local, specific and can be named. **T**/F

3. Killing in peaceful times is allowed.   T/**F**

4. Murder does not apply to declared war.
   T/F

5. People lose property and sounds of mirth and merriment during spiritual warfare.   T/**F**

6. Spiritual warfare is spiritual battle between the members of the Kingdom of God, on one side, and an extensive network of evil spiritual beings that are loyal to Satan, on the other side, which is fought in the realm of the spirit.
    T/F

7. Spiritual warfare is the partial displacement of satanic forces and the partial eradication and evacuation of the systems that ensure their survival.   T/**F**

8. The lies and falsehoods built in people's minds, can be demolished by teaching and preaching the truth of God's Word.   **T**/F

9. Satan can only win if we give him the opportunity to win.   **T**/F

10. Spiritual warfare is synonymous with strong, energetic declarations, heavy stamping of the feet or binding and loosening of the enemy.
    T/**F**

Essay-type Questions

1. List and explain the five (5) natural principles of spiritual warfare.

    [500 words or less].

2. Compare war to battle using biblical scriptures as a guide.

    [250 words or less].

3. Consider the three different definitions of spiritual warfare advanced in this book, namely:

    "Spiritual warfare is spiritual battle between the members of the Kingdom of God, on one side, and an extensive network of evil spiritual beings that are loyal to Satan, on the other side, which is fought in the realm of the spirit."

    "Spiritual warfare is a hostile contest between spiritual forces who are in a state of declared spiritual war, which is fought spiritually but whose effects manifest in the natural realm."

    "Spiritual warfare is the total displacement of satanic forces and the complete eradication and evacuation of the systems that ensure their survival."

In your opinion, explain what is central to all these definitions and in which way or ways are they different.

[1500 words or less].

4. Explain the grace-basis of spiritual warfare in reference to Romans 8:35-39.

[500 words or less].

34 | Levels of Spiritual Warfare

Multiple-choice Questions

1. Occult level spiritual warfare may also be called ____

    A. Strategic
    B. Magic
    C. Cosmic
    D. Ground

2. Which level of spiritual warfare has far-reaching impact against the Kingdom of God?

    A. Ground
    B. Magic
    C. Occult
    D. Strategic

3. Satan's ultimate strategy against God's people is to impose his lies through ____

    A. Belief systems
    B. Governments
    C. Possession
    D. Social media

4. Principalities at the strategic level may influence and determine all of these, except ___

   A. Customs
   B. Traditions
   C. Culture
   D. Revival

5. All of these may be part of the Strategic Maneuvers, except ___

   A. Research
   B. Spiritual mapping
   C. Familiar spirits
   D. Spiritual identification

6. Organized forces of darkness may include all these, except ___

   A. Witchcraft
   B. Shamanism
   C. Satanism
   D. Dominism

True/False Questions

1. Spiritual mapping happens when problem areas of a particular territory have the demonic activities there documented and recorded.   **T**/F

2. Spiritual identification may map the activities of familiar spirits.   **T**/F

3. Satan's chief strategy is to normalize evil.   **T**/F

4. The Lost Sheep Parable illustrates that, to God, one soul buffeted by demons may be His priority leaving the ninety-nine safe ones for later.   **T**/F

5. The weapon mostly used by satanic forces at strategic level is strongholds.   **T**/F

6. Paul encountered an occultic situation.   **T**/F

7. Ideology, social behavior and national legislation are the only means Satan uses to occupy territories.   T/**F**

8. Spiritual struggle is against flesh and blood.   T/**F**

9. Paul confronted Diana at the Island of Patmos.   T/**F**

10. A stationary spiritual ruler over a physical domain falls under the Concept of Territoriality.   **T**/F

Essay-type Questions

1. "For our struggle is not against flesh and blood, but against the rulers, against the authorities, against the powers of this dark world and against the spiritual forces of evil in the heavenly realms." Review this scripture in view of strategic level spiritual warfare.

   [500 words or less].

2. Define each of the following terms or phrases:

   a) Strategic-level intercession
   b) Strategic maneuvers
   c) Research in the history of the area
   d) Spiritual identification
   e) Familiar spirits
   f) Compulsory repentance

   [250 words or less].

35 | Demonology: An Introduction

Multiple-choice Questions

1. Who is the chief of demons?

   A. Satan
   B. Lucifer
   C. An archangel
   D. Principalities

2. Who/which of the following is at the same level as Satan?

   A. Jesus
   B. Powers
   C. Michael
   D. God

3. All these comprise the satanic hierarchy, except ____

   A. Principalities
   B. Satan
   C. Orders
   D. Rulers

4. Among Satan's arsenal is ___

   A. Songs
   B. Sin
   C. Trumpets
   D. Prayers

5. A/an ___ is a mindset impregnated with hopelessness that causes us to accept as unchallengeable, situations that we know are contrary to the will of God.

   A. Accusation
   B. Thought
   C. Stronghold
   D. Sin

True/False Questions

1. Satan's arsenal includes sin, accusations and strongholds.   **T**/F

2. Strongholds are triggered by speculations and assumptions, which are suppositions that cannot be proven.   **T**/F

3. "Good thoughts," are "godly thoughts."
    T/**F**

4. Satan targets our weaknesses. T/**F**

5. According to the Bible, masters shall receive greater condemnation.   **T**/F

6. Strongholds must be remodeled, repainted and covered.   T/**F**

7. Christians know very little about sin.
    T/**F**

8. Satan is a demon.   **T**/F

9. Satan has many names, many of which describe his nature and character.
    T/F

10. The end of Satan is the Lake of Fire.
    T/F

CHARLES MWEWA

Essay-type Questions

1. List at least ten (10) names of Satan.

   [250 words or less].

2. List and describe the five characteristics of strongholds.

   [500 words or less].

3. List and describe Satan's arsenal.

   [250 words or less].

4. Many, erroneously, compare Satan to God. Debunk the misunderstanding.

   [250 words or less].

36 | Demonology: The Delicate Web

Multiple-choice Questions

1. Spirit husbands are known in Latin as ___

   A. Succubus
   B. Incubus
   C. Wandering spirits
   D. Water spirits

2. Spirit wives are known in Latin as ___

   A. Succubus
   B. Incubus
   C. Wandering spirits
   D. Water spirits

3. Frequent sexual intercourse in dreams may be a ___

   A. Demonic presentation
   B. A physical spiritual spouse
   C. Masquerade
   D. Sign of fertility

4. Freedom over demonic presentation is a subject of ___

   A. Power
   B. Prayer
   C. Grace
   D. Glory

5. ___ is the final stage towards demonization.

   A. Repression
   B. Depression
   C. Obsession
   D. Possession

6. Suicidal thoughts/ideations may occur during ___

   A. Repression and suppression
   B. Depression and suppression
   C. Obsession and regression
   D. Possession and regression

7. Where a spiritual spouse is never satisfied with only one spouse, it may be a condition known as ___

   A. Succubus
   B. Spiritual prostitution
   C. Violent spirits
   D. Bathing in dreams

8. Spiritual spouses may impact ____

   A. Virtue
   B. Morals
   C. Achievement
   D. All of the above

9. Resident spirits may penetrate the human soul through ____

   A. Eyes
   B. Mouth
   C. Ears
   D. Genitals

10. Transference of spirits might have happened in the case of all of them, except ____

    A. Moses
    B. Elijah
    C. Paul
    D. John the Baptist

True/False Questions

1. Religious spirits or certain bad habits like lust, infidelity, to mention but a few, may be transferred through negative anointing.
   T/F

2. Libation is the pouring out of alcoholic beverages in the river to evoke the ancestral or familiar spirits.   **T**/F

3. Adultery, fornication and puberty rites are potential ways through which demons can get transferred.   **T**/F

4. Witchcraft, poverty, polygamy, prostitution, alcoholism, rates of divorce, hypertension, failure, chronic sickness may be hereditary.   **T**/F

5. Regression happens when a person begins to withdraw from reading God's Word and from prayer. **T**/F

6. Sleep-walking may, in rare instances, be a sign of blind witchcraft.   **T**/F

7. Late marriage is always a results of the demonic sexual affair. T/**F**

8. Marital conflicts are more often than not caused by demonic presentations.   T/**F**

9. Sex dreams always portend failure, calamity and non-achievement.   T/**F**

10. Grace has overcome all variants of demonic presentations.   **T**/F

Essay-type Questions

1. List and discuss the sources of demonization.

   [500 words or less].

2. List and discuss the stages of demonization.

   [500 words or less].

3. List and discuss at least five (5) variances of demonic activities.

   [500 or less words].

4. "Grace trumps over demonic influences." Discuss.

   [1500 words or less].

37 | Diabolical Spirits

Multiple-choice Questions

1. The "Queen of Heaven" belongs to an array of demonic spirits called ___

   A. Water spirits
   B. Mountain spirits
   C. Egyptian spirits
   D. Ba'al

2. Each of these gods is part of the "African Mythology," except ___

   A. Ra
   B. Isis
   C. Seth
   D. Athena

3. Mythological gods are seen in Christianity as ___

   A. Planets
   B. Stars
   C. Demons
   D. Good angels

4. The "Queen of Heaven" is worshipped by way of ____

   A. Altars
   B. Libation and altars
   C. Libation, altars and burning incense
   D. All of the above

5. Behind Pharaoh, king of Egypt, God saw ____

   A. A great monster (a demon)
   B. Iris
   C. Maker of River Nile
   D. Miracles

6. Through the "Queen of Heaven," Satan desires to be ____

   A. Immortal
   B. Invisible
   C. God
   D. Glorious

7. The "Queen of Heaven" may mean all these, except ____

   A. Without co-habitation
   B. Mother of sorrow
   C. One who dominates
   D. She who laughs

8. All these are characteristics of sorrow, except
____

   A. Fear of death
   B. Heaviness of heart
   C. Brokenness of spirit
   D. Joyous song

9. Iris means ____

   A. He who weeps
   B. She who weeps
   C. Weeping
   D. Sorrowful

10. Satan being crushed under believers' feet by the Lord, is ____

    A. Grace
    B. Sophistication
    C. True victory
    D. Awesome

True/False Questions

1. Water spirits are immoral.   **T**/F

2. Water spirits may cause ministry failure.
   T/F

3. The "Queen of Heaven" is Mary, the mother
   of Jesus.   T/**F**

4. The "Queen of Heaven" does not belong to
   water spirits.   T/**F**

5. The "Queen of Heaven" may break homes
   and marriages. **T**/F

6. The "Queen of Heaven" is master at the use
   of blackmail.   **T**/F

7. Libation is the same as drink offering. **T**/F

8. Under the guise of water spirits, sorrow may
   lead to depression.   **T**/F

9. The Book of Revelation provides a graphic
   demonstration of the final battle between the
   Church and the water spirits.   **T**/F

10. All the characteristics of the "Queen of
    Heaven" and of the water spirits in general,
    put together, cannot quench the zeal and
    thrust of the Church. **T**/F

Essay-type Questions

1. List and explain at least five (5) characteristics of water spirits.

    [500 words or less].

2. List and explain at least five (5) characteristics of the "Queen of Heaven."

    [500 words or less].

3. Differentiate between Ba'al and Beelzebub by using relevant scriptural references.

    [250 words or less].

4. In the context of grace and spiritual warfare, explain what the following verse of Scripture means: "And they have defeated him by the blood of the Lamb and by their testimony. And they did not love their lives so much that they were afraid to die."

    [500 words or less].

38 | Covenants

Multiple-choice Questions

1. Lovers who pledge to marry each other may enter into ____ covenants.

    A. Dream
    B. sexual
    C. Blood
    D. Mistakenly-made

2. Life is in the ____.

    A. Blood
    B. Brain
    C. Covenants
    D. Lies

3. Hidden covenants may also be known as ____ covenants.

    A. Dangerous
    B. Latent
    C. Mistakenly-made
    D. Flattery

4. All these are biblically and historically-made covenants, except ____

   A. Alamic
   B. Abrahamic
   C. Mosaic
   D. Davidic

5. The Old Testament was based on law; the New Covenant is based on ____

   A. Grace
   B. Regulations
   C. Faith
   D. Peace

6. You know a covenant is very serious if ____

   A. It is made of promises
   B. It is made by blood
   C. It is made between lesser and greater parties
   D. It involves close relatives

7. According to the Covenant of Redemption, the Father is the ____

   A. Designer
   B. Undertaker
   C. Applier
   D. Implementer

8. Who is the current federal head of the human race?

   A. Adam
   B. Eve
   C. Jesus Christ
   D. Both Adam and Eve

9. _____ is presumed under the Covenant of Grace.

   A. Love
   B. Peace
   C. Glory
   D. Faith

10. All the covenantal promises of God are of no effect unless ____

    A. They are actioned through prayer
    B. They are made with blood
    C. They are hidden covenants
    D. They are redemption in nature

True/False Questions

1. The dead are still alive and with us.   **T**/F

2. There is a life sharing in sexual covenants.
   T/F

3. It is possible to enter into a covenant by mistake.   **T**/F

4. Some people usually resort to misguided satanic practices to seek promotion, prosperity, fame, power, or protection.
   T/F

5. Reading palms and occult books, watching occultic films, playing ouija boards and practicing magic arts may be means through which some may be introduced into covenants.   **T**/F

6. Trespassing onto witch-doctors' houses may be one of the ways in which some people may enter into covenants.   **T**/F

7. Some families may pass on witchcraft trades by inheritance to the members of the family.
   T/F

8. Blood may be ritually combined with beer in covenant-entering rites.   **T**/F

9. There is an implied Covenant of Grace in the New Testament.   **T**/F

10. The benefits of who God is and what He has, have been made available to us by grace.
    T/F

Essay-type Questions

1. List and explain the three characteristics of blood covenants.

    [250 words or less].

2. Justify with the help of Scripture, the relationship among covenants, grace and prayer.

    [500 words or less].

3. Discuss the impact of committing adultery with a prostitute.

    [250 words or less].

39 | Curses

Multiple-choice Questions

1. Curses are direct opposites of ____

   A. Blessings
   B. Grace
   C. Sorrow
   D. Favor

2. All of these cannot be cursed, except ____

   A. Parents
   B. God
   C. Land
   D. The deaf

3. All these can be cursed, except ____

   A. Land
   B. Community
   C. The disobedient
   D. God's children

4. What abominable act attracted curses in the Old Testament and may still attract curses in the New Testament?

    A. Tithing
    B. Idolatry
    C. Sorcery
    D. Impertinence

5. Material blessings are defined as ___ under the dispensation of grace.

    A. Others
    B. Money
    C. Real wealth
    D. Land

6. All these are the elements of a curse, except ___

    A. Victim
    B. Enforcer
    C. Harm
    D. Blessings

7. The best counteractivity to cursing is ___

    A. Running away
    B. Striking back
    C. Speaking blessings to the declarant
    D. Speaking blessings to the victim

True/False Questions

1. God does not forbid people from cursing their rulers.   T/**F**

2. The deaf must be cursed.   T/**F**

3. Reuben, the firstborn of Israel, was never cursed.   T/**F**

4. Joshua did curse the city of Jericho.   T/**F**

5. Idolatry is silent in the New Testament.   T/**F**

6. Children called Elijah, " baldy!"   T/**F**

7. David was cursed because he killed Urea and married his wife, Bathsheba.   T/**F**

8. Truly born-again Christians can be cursed.   T/**F**

9. Under grace, curses are relative to one's state of righteousness.   T/**F**

10. True blessings can be purchased with money.   T/**F**

Essay-type Questions

1. List and explain all those who cannot be cursed according to Scripture.

   [250 words or less]

2. List and explain all those who can be cursed according to Scripture.

   [250 words or less]

3. "Grace has given us all things that pertain to life , wellbeing and godliness, among them lasting blessings that do not require money."

   a) Define spiritual blessings.
   b) Which prophet defined true blessings?
   c) List at least five (5) things that comprise physical/material blessings.
   d) Why has God stored true riches in the heavenlies?
   e) What is the view of money in relation to true wealth?

   [1500 words or less]

4. Discuss the importance of prayer in translating spiritual blessings into material blessings?

[250 words or less]

5. Define prosperity according to this chapter.

    [500 words or less].

6. List and describe at least ten (10) facets of the blessings of obedience tabulated in Deuteronomy 28.

    [500 words or less].

7. "Satan, the LORD rebuke thee, O Satan; even the LORD that hath chosen Jerusalem rebuke thee: is not this a brand." Discuss the use of language in spiritual warfare.

    [250 words or less].

8. Explain, with scriptural references, how to diffuse curses.

    [250 words or less].

9. List and define the elements of a curse.

    [250 words or less].

10. "Beze wakes up shackled to a bed by his father. Beze had taken his father's motor vehicle without his father's permission and caused an accident that led to the car being written off. The car had no insurance and Beze's father was very angry. In his anger,

Beze's father said, 'I wish you were not my son. May you never amount to anything till you die.' Beze thinks that what he had done did not warrant being tied to the bed for a week, denied a shower and food. Beze is heard saying, "My father just hates me. If it was Isaac, my young brother, he would have not tied him to the bed."'

Review the anecdote above and answer the following questions:

a) Was Beze cursed by his father?
b) Justify your answer in (a).
c) If Beze was cursed, how would he escape the effects of the curse?
d) If, in your opinion, Beze felt that his father' treatment of him was disproportionate and unfair, how would he deal with it if he were a Christian?

[1500 words or less].

40 | Exorcism

Multiple-choice Questions

1. Exorcism is ___

    A. Commanding spirits
    B. Chasing demons
    C. Casting out demons
    D. Taming spirits

2. Demon possession may be mistaken for all these, except___

    A. Demonization
    B. Emotional distress
    C. Multiple personality disorder
    D. Mental disorder

3. A Legion has at least ___ demons.

    A. 2,000
    B. 3,000
    C. 50,000
    D. 5,000

4. Legion means ___

   A. Many
   B. Romans
   C. Roman army
   D. Pigs

5. Our Lord's command of demons into pigs was an act of ___

   A. Desperation
   B. Animal cruelty
   C. Grace
   D. Wrath

6. All these may be characteristics of the demonic, except ___

   A. Multiple personality disorder
   B. Shouting loudly
   C. Reaction to Jesus' name
   D. Testability

7. All these may be components of the soul, except ___

   A. Mind
   B. Intellect
   C. Will
   D. Spirit

8. The part of a person that controls the sub-consciousness is the ___

   A. Spirit
   B. Soul
   C. Body
   D. Emotions

9. According to this chapter, the greatest fear of demons is ___

   A. Jesus Christ
   B. The Lake of Fire
   C. Women
   D. Commands

10. Exorcism is ___

   A. Ground level spiritual warfare
   B. Strategic level spiritual warfare
   C. Occult level spiritual warfare
   D. Counseling level spiritual warfare

True/False Questions

1. Only one demon can possess a person at a time.   T/**F**

2. Total demon possession does not harm the spirituality of a person.   T/**F**

3. Pigs are a symbol of evil.   T/**F**

4. Demons can't return into an individual once they are casted out.   T/**F**

5. Demons easily confess that Jesus Christ is Lord.   T/**F**

6. Exorcism is the process of expelling or the casting out of the devil himself from an individual.   T/**F**

7. A demon-possessed person is called the counsellor, while the person conducting exorcism is called the counselee.   T/**F**

8. The authority to cast out demons comes only from Jesus Christ.   **T**/F

9. Exorcism is an operation of grace.   **T**/F

10. Demons can lead people or animals to death.   **T**/F

Essay-type Questions

1. List and describe three characteristics that may suggest the presence of the demonic.

    [250 words or less].

2. Summarize the process of exorcism.

    [500 words or less].

3. State other ways, in addition to prayer and fasting, a person must do in order to prepare for exorcism.

    [500 or less words].

4. Jesus said: "But if I drive out demons by the finger of God, then the Kingdom of God has come upon you" (Luke 11:20). Explain this verse of Scripture in relation to grace and exorcism.

    [500 words or less].

41 | Deliverance

Multiple-choice Questions

1. ___ is the bringing of somebody out of the captivity of the devil or demons.

   A. Deliverance
   B. Exorcism
   C. Denunciation
   D. Restitution

2. ___ is the rejection or leaving of the evil spirits working against you.

   A. Deliverance
   B. Renunciation
   C. Denunciation
   D. Restitution

3. ___ is the aspect of paying back in compensation for what was taken.

   A. Deliverance
   B. Renunciation
   C. Denunciation
   D. Restitution

4. People may be delivered from all these, except ___

   A. Fruitlessness
   B. Barrenness
   C. Infertility
   D. Productivity

5. What actualizes renunciation?

   A. Renunciation
   B. Restitution
   C. Reproduction
   D. Reinvention

True/False Questions

1. To repent is to turn away from something or someone and to return to God   **T**/F

2. Repentance can happen without confessing sins.   T/**F**

3. Demons may sire symbolic spiritual children with humans.   **T**/F

4. The destruction of anything physical that connects one to the demoniacs may be a vital part of renunciation.   **T**/F

5. Grace gives us the power in Christ to decree all we may need in order to free us from demonic interference, influence or even possession.   **T**/F

Essay-type Questions

1. "And they overcame him by the blood of the lamb and by the word of their testimony; and they loved not their lives unto the death."

   a) Who is "they" in this scriptural verse?
   b) Who is "him" in this scriptural verse?
   c) Who is the "lamb" in this verse?
   d) Define the three levels of spiritual engagement.
   e) How does the three levels of spiritual engagement relate to the three levels of spiritual warfare, if any?

   [1500 words or less]

2. "[14] Stand firm then, with the belt of truth buckled around your waist, with the breastplate of righteousness in place, [15] and with your feet fitted with the readiness that comes from the Gospel of peace. [16] In addition to all this, take up the shield of faith, with which you can extinguish all the flaming arrows of the evil one. [17] Take the helmet of salvation and the sword of the Spirit, which is the word of God."

   Review this passage of Scripture and relate it to the degree of readiness impressed upon a Roman solder equipped for battle.

   [500 words or less].

42 | Offensive Weapons

Multiple-choice Questions

1. What is the reason that Jesus Christ came?

   A. To destroy the works of the devil
   B. To redeem the damned
   C. To save the lost
   D. All of the above are correct

2. _____ is a helmet.

   A. Salvation
   B. Righteousness
   C. Truth
   D. Word of God

3. ___ is the breastplate.

   A. Salvation
   B. Righteousness
   C. Truth
   D. Word of God

4. ___ is the shield.

   A. Salvation
   B. Righteousness
   C. Truth
   D. Word of God

5. ___ is the sword.

   A. Salvation
   B. Righteousness
   C. Truth
   D. Word of God

6. The blood of Jesus Christ is a believer's ___ weapon.

   A. Offensive
   B. Defensive
   C. Divine
   D. Spiritual

7. Righteousness is the believer's ___weapon.

   A. Offensive
   B. Defensive
   C. Divine
   D. Spiritual

True/False Questions

1. The name of Jesus is what gives power to our weaponry.   **T**/F

2. The name of Jesus is the power of attorney.   **T**/F

3. Without the name of Jesus, our weapons, though potentially powerful, will be blunt.   **T**/F

4. Our offensive and defensive weapons put together have tremendous power to demolish Satan's arsenal.   **T**/F

5. Satan's arsenal includes sin, accusations and strongholds.   **T**/F

6. Some of our defensive weaponry are righteousness, truth, salvation and faith.   **T**/F

7. Some of our offensive weapons are the blood of Jesus, our testimony and our allegiance to God.   **T**/F

8. Spiritual rules of engagements exist and they are respected by Satan.   T/**F**

9. The Word of God has the power.   **T**/F

10. The three levels of spiritual engagement are power, truth and allegiance.   **T**/F

Essay-type Questions

1. "And they overcame him by the blood of the lamb and by the word of their testimony; and they loved not their lives unto the death."

   f) Who is "they" in this scriptural verse?
   g) Who is "him" in this scriptural verse?
   h) Who is the "lamb" in this verse?
   i) Define the three levels of spiritual engagement.
   j) How does the three levels of spiritual engagement relate to the three levels of spiritual warfare, if any?

   [1500 words or less]

2. "[14] Stand firm then, with the belt of truth buckled around your waist, with the breastplate of righteousness in place, [15] and with your feet fitted with the readiness that comes from the Gospel of peace. [16] In addition to all this, take up the shield of faith, with which you can extinguish all the flaming arrows of the evil one. [17] Take the helmet of salvation and the sword of the Spirit, which is the word of God."

   Review this passage of Scripture and relate it to the degree of readiness impressed upon a Roman solder equipped for battle.

   [500 words or less].

43 | The Heavenlies

Multiple-choice Questions

1. Spiritual warfare in heavenly places is called ___

   A. Cosmic warfare
   B. Heavenlies
   C. Strategic
   D. Heavenly places

2. The heavenlies are the ___ realm of our present world.

   A. Second
   B. Third
   C. Fourth
   D. Tertiary

3. In spiritual warfare parlance, hell is the ___

   A. Cosmic grave
   B. Ephemeral grace
   C. Fourth heavens
   D. Up above

4. Satan and demons occupy the earth by way of
____

    A. Human embodiment
    B. Animal embodiment
    C. Human possession
    D. All of the above

5. The heavenly place is the storehouse of ____

    A. Blessings
    B. Warfare
    C. Demons
    D. Arsenal

6. What do we call the body of Christian believers who gather together anywhere in the name of Jesus Christ?

    A. Church
    B. The Body of Christians
    C. A Christian Mosque
    D. Ecclesia

7. The outcomes of salvation include all these, except ____

    A. Saved souls
    B. Healed bodies
    C. Delivered persons
    D. Defeated church

8. All these belong to Heaven1, except ____

    A. The sun
    B. The moon
    C. The 24 elders
    D. The stars

9. All these belong to earth, except ____

    A. Dragons
    B. Deeps
    C. Deserts and mountains
    D. Angels

10. Hell is usually confused with ___

    A. Hades
    B. The Lake of Fire
    C. Deep seas
    D. Heaven

11. The Gates of Hell are a symbol of ___

    A. Hell
    B. Powers of darkness
    C. Dominions
    D. Entry point

12. Who is the Head of the Church?

    A. The Pope
    B. The Holy Spirit
    C. The Lord Jesus Christ
    D. God, the Father

True/False Questions

1. The existence of Hell is understood, but the location of Hell has eluded many a Bible scholar.   **T**/F

2. Hell is the same as the Lake of Fire.   T/**F**

3. Hell is more like a temporary detention than a permanent prison sentence.   **T**/F

4. Satan and demons can still have influence on earth from Hell.   **T**/F

5. Satan and demons can influence people on earth directly from Hell without the use of a medium.   T/**F**

6. Hell is somewhere in heaven, and, hence, the name cosmic grave.   T/**F**

7. Sometimes, the best way to understand the meaning of Scripture is with the aid of literary techniques.   **T**/F

8. "The realm of the dead," refers to Hell.   **T**/F

9. The Lake of Fire is the end of all satanic and demonic activities.   **T**/F

10. Hell seems to be a place of grief, mourning, misery, sorrow, sadness, anguish, and pain.   **T**/F

Essay-type Questions

1. With the help of scriptural references from the Book of Ephesians, dissect the philosophy behind the heavenlies.

    [1,500 words or less].

2. Define the Church, and explain its purpose in relation to the destruction of the Kingdom of Darkness.

    [500 words or less].

3. Differentiate the earth and the heavenlies as respective battlefields in relation to the levels of spiritual warfare discussed in Chapter 33.

    [500 words or less].

44 | Tongues and Spiritual Warfare

Multiple-choice Questions

1. Praying in the spirit should be ____

   A. Occasionally
   B. At all time
   C. When we feel like
   D. When we don't feel like

2. To quench the Holy Spirit is all these, except ____

   A. Stifle
   B. Extinguish
   C. Restrain or put out
   D. Energize

3. When we pray in unknown tongues, we ____ Jesus.

   A. Glorify
   B. Dodge
   C. Elude
   D. Excite

4. "Abba" means ___

   A. Father
   B. Mother
   C. Intimacy
   D. Promise

5. Slavery leads to all these, except ___

   A. Freedom
   B. Fear
   C. Bondage
   D. A broken spirit

6. When our spirit prays in another language, it is an act of ___

   A. Grace
   B. Faith
   C. Goodness
   D. Power

7. As it regards intercession, the Holy Spirit brings us ___ to respond to God's immediate need for prayer to be answered.

   A. Promptings
   B. Weeping
   C. Groanings
   D. Laughs

True/False Questions

1. Praying in tongues is praying the will of God into action through the power that is contained in the name of Jesus Christ, our Lord.   **T**/F

2. Praying in the spirit is holistic.   **T**/F

3. Speaking in tongues is an offensive weapon of spiritual warfare and is an extension of the authority Jesus, our Lord, gave to us in His name. **T**/F

4. The Holy Spirit is God.   **T**/F

5. An advocate is the same as a lawyer.   **T**/F

6. God has adopted us through His Spirit into slaves. T/**F**

7. praying in other tongues leads to defeat.   T/**F**

8. The Holy Spirit helps us in our strengths.   T/**F**

9. Tongues are for Pentecostals alone.   T/**F**

10. Azrael is believed to be the archangel of life.
T/**F**

Essay-type Questions

1. List and explain the six ways in which speaking in tongues (other languages) activates the power of the Holy Spirit.

    [1,500 words or less].

45 | Angels' Ministry

Multiple-choice Questions

1. _____ is the study of angels.

   A. Angelology
   B. Demonology
   C. Exorcism
   D. Satanism

2. The two broad categories of angels are ___

   A. Cherubim and seraphim
   B. Elohim and seraphim
   C. Cherubim and Elohim
   D. Moses and Elijah

3. Archangel Gabriel is a/an ___

   A. Seraphim
   B. Cherubim
   C. Angel who conquered Lucifer
   D. 24th elder

"In the year that King Uzziah died I saw the Lord sitting upon a throne, high and lifted up; and the train of his robe filled the temple. Above him stood the seraphim. Each had six wings: with two he covered his face, and with two he covered his feet, and with two he flew. And one called to another and said: 'Holy, holy, holy is the Lord of hosts; the whole earth is full of his glory!' And the foundations of the thresholds shook at the voice of him who called, and the house was filled with smoke. And I said: 'Woe is me! For I am lost; for I am a man of unclean lips, and I dwell in the midst of a people of unclean lips; for my eyes have seen the King, the Lord of hosts!'" (Isaiah 6:1-13).

Answer questions 4 and 5 based on this passage:

4. Who is narrating the story?

   A. Isaiah
   B. God
   C. An angel
   D. King Uzziah

5. Why does the narrator take it for granted that the angel he saw was a seraphim?

   A. Because it had six wings
   B. Because the angel covered the face
   C. Because the angel worshipped God
   D. The foundations of the thresholds shook

6. If in the beginning God made one trillion angelic beings, what would be the number of holy angels now?

   A. About 666,666,666,667
   B. About 333,333,333,333
   C. A myriad
   D. Infinitum

7. All these may be territorial princes, except ___

   A. Prince of Persia
   B. Prince of Greece
   C. The beasts at Ephesus
   D. The Mayor of Catharge

8. Nyami-nyami is likely the principality over ___

   A. Southern Zambia
   B. Northern Zambia
   C. Malawi
   D. Northern Angola

9. What is the central difference between good or holy angels and demons?

   A. Angels don't marry
   B. Demons do possess people
   C. Angels obey every Word of God
   D. Demons obey every Word of God

10. In the Bible, dragon may refer to Satan or to a/an ____

    A. Demon
    B. Angel
    C. Whale
    D. Chinese gods

11. Who is the Prince of Israel?

    A. Adam
    B. Michael
    C. Gabriel
    D. David

12. In the Old Testament, God called angels His sons, and human beings His ____

    A. Daughters
    B. Works [of His hands]
    C. Creatures
    D. Pride

True/False Questions

1. Angels are created beings but demons and Satan are not.   T/**F**

2. Angels worship the Living God but demons and Satan dare to disobey Him. **T**/F

3. Angels make the Word of God effective by doing God's pleasure.   **T**/F

4. Angels deliver and defend the saints in conflict between good and evil.   **T**/F

5. Angels cause the saints to walk in evil-free paths and they form a permanent fence for their security.   **T**/F

6. Human beings may command God of things concerning angels.   **T**/F

7. Michael and angels were responsible for evicting Satan and his demons from Heaven.   **T**/F

8. In order to release angels to work for us, only knowledge but not confidence is vital.   T/**F**

9. Elijah prayed, "Open his eyes, Lord, so that he may see."   T/**F**

10. "Ask me of things to come concerning my sons, and concerning the works of my hands command me" is quintessentially about prayer.   **T**/F

Essay-type Questions

1. Discuss the consideration one must take into account to release angels.

   [500 words or less].

2. "In general, we are more ignorant of territorial holy angels than we are of demons." Discuss using contemporary examples.

   [250 words or less].

3. Define Angelology, and provide biblical examples to highlight ways in which angels operate.

   [1,500 words or less].

46 | Spiritual Warfare and Counseling

Multiple-choice Questions

1. ISA stands for ____

   A. Independent spiritual advice
   B. Interdependent spiritual advice
   C. Indiscreet spiritual advice
   D. Independent satanic activities

2. All these constitute the three essential conditions of counseling, except ____

   A. Acceptance
   B. Reassurance
   C. Confidentiality
   D. Competence

3. The aim of ____ is to help the counselee move from a state of brokenness towards wholeness.

   A. Counseling
   B. Coaching
   C. Deliverance
   D. Negative experience

4. What are the long-term goals of counseling?

   A. Removing symptoms
   B. Restoring to earlier levels of functionality
   C. Freeing the persons to reach their potential
   D. All of the above

5. The quality of empathy in counseling is akin to ___

   A. Dependability
   B. Genuineness
   C. Frugality
   D. Confidentiality

True/False Questions

1. During counseling, attack the problem and the person.   T/**F**

2. Cases of confidentiality would normally include cases in which the counselee appears to be a danger to themselves and to others.   **T**/F

3. Most often, people come to counseling asking for help, while they are fully persuaded in their heart of hearts that it will help them.   T/**F**

4. For real healing of hurting people to take place, the counselor must be aware of the process by which counseling is carried out. **T**/F

5. In spiritual counseling involving satanic or demonic forces, long-term goals should not involve a plan to study God's Word and learn how to pray. T/**F**

Essay-type Questions

1. List and describe the three conditions of counseling.

   [250 words or less].

2. List and describe the three qualities of successful counseling.

   [250 words or less].

3. Describe the spiritual nature of counseling in a case involving a formerly demon possessed individual.

   [500 words or less].

47 | Concept of Revival

Multiple-choice Questions

Multiple-choice questions are based on the following passage in Ezekiel:

37 The hand of the LORD was on me, and he brought me out by the Spirit of the LORD and set me in the middle of a valley; it was full of bones. ² He led me back and forth among them, and I saw a great many bones on the floor of the valley, bones that were very dry. ³ He asked me, "Son of man, can these bones live?" I said, "Sovereign LORD, you alone know." ⁴ Then he said to me, "Prophesy to these bones and say to them, 'Dry bones, hear the word of the LORD! ⁵ This is what the Sovereign LORD says to these bones: I will make breath[a] enter you, and you will come to life. ⁶ I will attach tendons to you and make flesh come upon you and cover you with skin; I will put breath in you, and you will come to life. Then you will know that I am the LORD.'" ⁷ So I prophesied as I was commanded. And as I was prophesying, there was a noise, a rattling sound, and the bones came together, bone to bone. ⁸ I looked, and tendons and flesh appeared on them and skin covered them, but there was no breath in them. ⁹ Then he said to me, "Prophesy to the breath; prophesy, son of man, and say to it, 'This is what the Sovereign LORD says: Come, breath, from the four winds and breathe into these slain, that they may live.'" ¹⁰ So I prophesied as he commanded me, and breath entered them; they came to life and stood up on their feet—a vast army. (Ezekiel 37:1-10).

1. Who is the "Spirit of the LORD" in this passage?

    A. The Holy Spirit
    B. The human spirit
    C. Jesus Christ
    D. God

2. "Bones" are a symbol of ___

    A. Dead animals
    B. The Church
    C. Israel
    D. Both (B) and (C) are correct

3. "…bones that were very dry," alludes to ___

    A. A dead Jerusalem
    B. A dead Church
    C. A well roasted lamb
    D. A lukewarm Israel

4. The injunction, "Prophesy to these bones and say to them, 'Dry bones, hear the word of the LORD…'" describes ___

    A. Prayer of weeping
    B. Prayer of groaning
    C. Mountain moving prayer
    D. Prayer of power

5. The statement, "I will make breath enter you, and you will come to life" defines ___

    A. Israel
    B. The Church
    C. Revival
    D. Victory

6. The statement, "And as I was prophesying, there was a noise, a rattling sound, and the bones came together, bone to bone" speaks of two agents, which are these?

    A. Prayer and grace
    B. Prayer and Holy Spirit power
    C. Prayer and sounds of joy
    D. Prayer and speaking in tongues

7. The phrase, "I looked…" may describe which injunction given by the Lord in relation to prayer?

    A. Watching
    B. Fasting
    C. Praising
    D. Dreaming

8. The statement, "Come, breath, from the four winds and breathe into these slain, that they may live," may denote that revival cannot happen without ___

    A. A whirlwind
    B. The Holy Spirit
    C. Prayer
    D. Life

9. The phrase, "So I prophesied as he commanded me…" may connote ___

    A. That revival requires obedience
    B. That revivals may be inspired by God
    C. That revivals involve prayer
    D. All of the above

10. The phrase, "…and breath entered them; they came to life and stood up on their feet—a vast army," defines ___

    A. Purpose of a revival
    B. The foundation of revival
    C. The spirit of a revival
    D. The spiritual nature of a revival

True/False Questions

1. The Holy Spirit is an "It".   T/**F**

2. There are approximately 26 titles of the Holy Spirit in the New Testament Bible.
   T/**F**

3. Pneumatology is the study of the Spirit.
   T/F

4. The Holy Spirit has no distinct personality in the Godhead.   T/**F**

5. The Holy Spirit is Lord.   **T**/F

6. The Holy Spirit is also the Spirit of grace.
   T/F

7. Omnipotent means all-knowing.   T/**F**

8. Wine is forbidden in the Bible.   T/**F**

9. The Holy Spirit is compared to wind, and wind stands for the breath of life.
   T/F

10. Prayer and revival cause each other.   **T**/F

11. The Holy Spirit is the Spirit of both grace and prayer.   **T**/F

12. *Oinos* is the best suited definition of the Greek word "wine" comparable in New Testament Christianity.   T/**F**

Essay-type Questions

1. List and discuss at least 20 titles of the Holy Spirit.

   [1,500 words or less].

2. List and describe at least two attributes of the Holy Spirit.

   [250 words or less].

3. Define pneumatology and locate the Holy Spirit in the Godhead structure.

   [250 words or less].

4. List and describe at least four characteristics of wine, and explain how related they are to the effect of the in-filling of the Holy Spirit.

   [500 words or less].

5. Establish a relation among prayer, grace and revival, and explain why all are needed to have an effective Church.

   [1,000 words or less].

48 | The Anointing and Prayer

Multiple-choice Questions

1. The The prescriptive connotation of the anointing informs ___

   A. Its application
   B. Its description
   C. Its definition
   D. Its conceptualization

2. The anointing involves at least three factors.

   A. The source, the instrument and the recipient
   B. The giver, the receiver and the source
   C. The recipient, the receiver, and the giver
   D. The recipient, the agent and the source

3. The ___ is the essence of the Holy Spirit.

   A. Enablement
   B. Endorsement
   C. Empowerment
   D. Endearment

4. Each of these may be the form in each the enablement manifests, except ___

   A. Hope
   B. Abilities
   C. Talents
   D. Callings

5. One of these is a function of an anointing.

   A. Setting apart
   B. Sanctification
   C. Redemption
   D. Salvation

6. The New Testament follows after the ___ anointing.

   A. Melchizedek
   B. Aaron
   C. Levitical
   D. Canonical

7. The anointing does each of these, except ___

   A. It makes people speak in tongues
   B. It transforms recipients into different people
   C. The Holy Spirit works mightily in such people
   D. It endorses with geniuses

8. _____ was used as the symbol of the _____

    A. Oil; Holy Spirit
    B. Oil; anointing
    C. Laying on of hands; anointing
    D. Laying on of hands; oil

9. What is the meaning of the irrevocability of God's gifts, including the anointing?

    A. God can't take them back
    B. God can take them back
    C. They are temporary bequeathments
    D. Sin ends their existence

10. What is assumed in this statement: "Jesus Christ was uniquely anointed."

    A. That the anointing is individualized
    B. That the anointing is general in nature
    C. That Jesus' anointing applies to every believer
    D. That Jesus can lose His anointing.

True/False Questions

1. The There is a unique transformation when imparted with the anointing   **T**/F

2. The OT anointing foreshadowed the ministry of grace.   **T**/F

3. The anointing is the same thing as the in-filling, in-dwelling of the Holy Spirit.   T/**F**

4. Prayer brings the anointing.   **T**/F

5. Lucifer, Samson, King Saul and Ichabod all justify the irrevocability of God's anointing (callings).   **T**/F

6. Grace is the same as favor.   T/**F**

7. Hardships and negative circumstances diminish the anointing. T/**F**

8. Oil on its own is impotent; it is the Holy Spirit-infused prayer that gives it the unique anointing power.   **T**/F

9. The Holy Spirit and power are always present when a person is operating under an anointing.   **T**/F

10. Only elders can heal the sick in the name of Jesus Christ.   T/**F**

Essay-type Questions

1. The James 5:14-16 seems to suggest that the elders' prayer of faith accompanied by anointing with oil in the name of Jesus can cause those people's sins to be forgiven. Discuss.

   [500 words or less].

2. Distinguish grace from favor.

   [500 words or less].

3. What does the idea of a holy-priesthood show?

   [500 words or less].

4. Review 1 Samuel 21. How did the kingly anointing compliment the priestly anointing? How does the concept of grace feature into David-Ahimelek encounter at Nob?

   [1000 words or less].

5. Discuss the different uses of oil in the Bible.

   [500 words or less].

49 | Prayer and Church Growth

Multiple-choice Questions

1. Church growth must be defined in relation to all these, except ____

   A. Organizational complexity
   B. Quality
   C. Effectiveness
   D. Quantity

2. A church may be classified in terms of all of the following, except ____

   A. Its expansion
   B. Its position
   C. Its extension
   D. Its bridging effect

3. Jesus said to them, "Go into all the world and preach the gospel to every creature. Whoever believes and is baptized will be saved, but whoever does not believe will be condemned" (Mark 16:15-16). Which class of church growth is depicted in this order?

   A. Quality
   B. Bridging
   C. Teleological
   D. Quantity

4. The other name for bridging growth is ___

   A. Commissioning growth
   B. Organizational growth
   C. Purity growth
   D. Quality growth

5. "Those who believed what Peter said were baptized and added to the church that day—about 3,000 in all" (Acts 2:36-42, see 41). What class of church growth happened in this context?

   A. Expansion growth
   B. Extension growth
   C. Bridging growth
   D. Internal growth

6. "While they were worshiping the Lord and fasting, the Holy Spirit said, 'Set apart for Me Barnabas and Saul for the work to which I have called them.' And after they had fasted and prayed, they laid their hands on them and sent them off," (Acts 13:2-3). What class of church growth happened in this context?

   A. Expansion growth
   B. Extension growth
   C. Bridging growth
   D. Internal growth

7. "They devoted themselves to the apostles' teaching and to the fellowship, to the breaking of bread and to prayer. A sense of awe came over everyone, and the apostles performed many wonders and signs," (Acts 2:42-43). What class of church growth happened in this context?

   A. Expansion growth
   B. Extension growth
   C. Bridging growth
   D. Internal growth

8. What is the other name for internal growth?

   A. Quality
   B. Quantity
   C. Bridging
   D. Commissioning

9. This class of growth happens where there is a significant difference in terms of culture, race, language or socio-economic status with the originating church.

   A. Quality
   B. Quantity
   C. Bridging
   D. Commissioning

10. "Now in the church at Antioch there were prophets and teachers: Barnabas, Simeon called Niger, Lucius of Cyrene, Manaen (who had been brought up with Herod the tetrarch)

and Saul. While they were worshiping the Lord and fasting, the Holy Spirit said, 'Set apart for me Barnabas and Saul for the work to which I have called them.' So, after they had fasted and prayed, they placed their hands on them and sent them off," (Acts 13:1-3). This type of collaboration explains ____

A. **Organizational complexity**
B. Ministration compromise
C. Evangelistic precogitation
D. Missionary ingenuity

True/False Questions

1. Teleological growth and internal growth mean the same thing. **T**/F

2. Elders and deacons are members of the fivefold ministers. T/**F**

3. The fivefold ministers are apostles, prophets, evangelists, pastors and teachers. **T**/F

4. Church leaders are never burned out because they have the power of the Holy Spirit in them. T/**F**

5. Prayer is irrelevant to church growth. T/**F**

6. The Church is a living organization.
   T/F

7. There is something like having the right leaders in the right leadership positions in churches.   **T**/F

8. Prayer is the only weapon we have in the Church.   T/**F**

9. Prayer generates spiritual power for church growth.**T**/F

10. The Kingdom of Heaven is in a state of violence.   T/**F**

Essay-type Questions

1. "And he gave some, apostles; and some, prophets; and some, evangelists; and some, pastors and teachers; for the perfecting of the saints, for the work of the ministry, for the edifying of the body of Christ: Till we all come in the unity of the faith, and of the knowledge of the Son of God, unto a perfect man, unto the measure of the stature of the fulness of Christ" (Ephesians 4:11-13).

   Explain this passage in relation to the impact of leadership on church growth.
   [500 words or less].

2. "But when Peter came to Antioch, I opposed
    him in public, because he was clearly wrong.
    Before some men who had been sent by
    James arrived there, Peter had been eating
    with the Gentiles believers. But after these
    men arrived, he drew back and would not eat
    with the Gentiles, because he was afraid of
    those who were in favor of circumcising
    them. The other Jewish believers also started
    acting like cowards along with Peter; and even
    Barnabas was swept along by their cowardly
    action. When I saw that they were not walking
    a straight path in line with the truth of the
    gospel, I said to Peter in front of them all,
    "You are a Jew, yet you have been living like a
    Gentiles, not like a Jew. How, then, can you
    try to force Gentiles to live like Jews?"
    (Galatians 2:11-14).

    Using all the knowledge you have acquired in
    this chapter, discuss the above passage, by
    giving relevant examples.

    [1,500 words or less].

50 | Principles of Public Prayer

Multiple-choice Questions

1. All these apply to public prayer, except ____

   A. Preparation
   B. Sensitive
   C. Unspiritual
   D. Prayer leader

2. A place of the public prayer meeting is called
   ____

   A. Venue
   B. Cathedral
   C. Synagogue
   D. Rally

3. "The continuous flow of the prayer meeting from request to request until the meeting is done" defines ____

   A. Progression
   B. Spiritual wavelength
   C. Wave-tone
   D. Prayer items

Answer questions 4 to 6 based on the passage below:

"And Ezra the priest brought the law before the congregation both of men and women, and all that could hear with understanding, upon the first day of the seventh month. And he read therein before the street that was before the water gate from the morning until midday, before the men and the women, and those that could understand; and the ears of all the people were attentive unto the book of the law. And Ezra the scribe stood upon a pulpit of wood, which they had made for the purpose.... And Ezra opened the book in the sight of all the people; (for he was above all the people); and when he opened it, all the people stood up: And Ezra blessed the LORD, the great God. And all the people answered, Amen, Amen, with lifting up their hands: and they bowed their heads and worshiped the LORD with their faces to the ground" (Nehemiah 8:2-6).

    4. In this passage, Ezra is the ___

      A. Prayer leader
      B. Grand Master
      C. Volunteer
      D. Cheerleader

5. In the statement, "And Ezra the scribe stood upon a pulpit of wood, which they had made for the purpose," a pulpit of wood is the ___

    A. Prayer rostrum
    B. Prayer docket
    C. Prayer book
    D. Prayer request

6. The phrase, "And he read therein before the street…And all the people answered, Amen, Amen," denotes a ___

    A. Public prayer
    B. Street betting
    C. Public showoff
    D. Large crowd

7. All these are forms of preparations required in conducting a successful public prayer meeting, except ___

    A. Grandstanding
    B. Physical
    C. Spiritual
    D. Personal

8. What establishes the mood of a public prayer meeting?

   A. Spiritual wavelength
   B. The prayer leader
   C. The items carefully selected for the meeting
   D. A committee of experts

9. All these are indexes of a successful public prayer meeting, except ____

   A. Dagos
   B. Pathos
   C. Ethos
   D. Logos

10. What is the purpose of making an eloquently beautiful and sweet prayer in public?

    A. It glorifies God
    B. It dignifies God
    C. It settles and attracts the audience's attention
    D. All of the above

11. In public praying, the domain is ____

    A. Subject to a variety of expectations
    B. Private
    C. A vacuum
    D. Antisocial

12. The immediate benefit of a public prayer meeting is ___

    A. Praiseful inducement
    B. Answer to prayers
    C. A sense of unity
    D. All of the above

True/False Questions

1. Public praying is anti-New Testament.
    T/**F**

2. The leader of the prayer meeting is also its emcee.   **T**/F

3. In conducting a public prayer meeting, personal preparation is more important than either spiritual or physical preparations.
    T/**F**

4. Worship is not very important to public prayer.   T/**F**

5. Auxiliaries can start at any wavelength they so desire.   T/**F**

6. In conducting public prayer meetings, the prayer and the prayor must be one and the same.   **T**/F

7. The emotive content of the prayer is also known as logos. T/**F**

8. The prayer leader must not be punctual; the auxiliaries can do the job. T/**F**

9. There is a relationship between the prayer of agreement and public prayer. **T**/F

10. Public praying relates directly to national days of prayer proclaimed in some countries. **T**/F

Essay-type Questions

1. Define the following terms:

   a) Auxiliaries
   b) EMCEE
   c) Ethos
   d) Logos
   e) Pathos
   f) Personal preparation
   g) Physical preparation
   h) Prayer docket
   i) Prayer items (prayer requests)
   j) Prayer leader
   k) Prayer rostrum
   l) Progression
   m) Spiritual preparation
   n) Spiritual wavelength
   o) Venue

   [1,500 words or less].

51 | Hints on Setting Up a Prayer Ministry

Multiple-choice Questions

1. All these be involved in a business, except ___

    A. Occupation
    B. Profession
    C. Trade
    D. Prayer

2. The prayer leader managing a prayer department may be called ___

    A. Prayer pastor
    B. Elder in charge of prayer
    C. Prayer coordinator
    D. All of the above

3. The prayer department must ___

    A. Be managed
    B. Be coordinated
    C. Left to chance
    D. Both (A) and (B) are correct

4. Any of these can suffice as a prayer room ___

    A. Church building
    B. Mountains
    C. Home
    D. All of the above

5. The prayer coordinator must ___

    A. Be autonomous so that they can receive dreams and visions
    B. Be very educated so that they can manage effectively
    C. Be faithful to God, willing to learn and loyal to God and church leadership
    D. Be good at praying that everyone opens their eyes when they stand to pray

True/False Questions

1. All one needs is a college degree to set up and manage a prayer department.   T/**F**

2. Church is a living organization and a prayer ministry within it must also be a living organization.   **T**/F

3. The pastor of the church cannot be the coordinator of prayer in the same church in which they pastor.   T/**F**

4. Church must centralize prayer leadership across the board.   T/**F**

5. At the minimum, a leader of a prayer department must know how to delegate, garner logistical support, document as record the operations of the department, and lead in prayer.   **T**/F

6. Once a strong prayer ministry exists in the church, it will reduce the load off the pastor, thereby allowing them to enjoy coffee.   T/**F**

7. Record keeping in itself is a dynamic source of thanksgiving in later times. **T**/F

8. During the general prayer meetings which involve a large group of people or the entire church, the coordinator and the pastor of the church should lead the prayers.   **T**/F

9. A prayer room must be kept clean and neat.   **T**/F

10. A prayer room must be accessible, but with safeguards in place to ensure the health, safety and security of everyone involved.   **T**/F

Essay-type Questions

1. List and discuss the eight hints needed to set up a thriving and successful church prayer department.

    [1,500 words or less].

52 | Prayer and Technology

Multiple-choice Questions

1. What does the use of prayer technologies reveal?

   A. The will of God
   B. The grace of God
   C. The mercy of God
   D. The wisdom of God

2. What is technology?

   A. It is an invention
   B. It is an invention that helps to solve problems
   C. It is an invention that helps to solve people's problems
   D. It is an invention that makes it easier to solve people's problems

3. Any one of them, used technology to enhance God's agenda, except:

   A. Moses
   B. Solomon
   C. Cain
   D. Eve

4. Each of these is a prayer app, except:

   A. Abide
   B. Daily prayer guide
   C. My daily prayer and devotion
   D. Games of prayer guides

5. Which of the following is one of the benefits of a prayer app?

   A. Great source of being alone with God
   B. Great source of changing natural forces
   C. Ideal tool of teaching on fasting
   D. Ideal tool of sharing Gospel truths

True/False Questions

1. Prayer apps are a recent phenomenon. **T**/F

2. The Bible is devoid of technological examples.   T/**F**

3. Technology is anything that solves people's problems quickly.   T/**F**

4. Prayer apps underestimate our conversations with God   T/**F**

5. Prayer can benefit from technology.   **T**/F

6. Prayer is the most important affair of the day.
   T/F

7. Prayer technology makes it easier for us to know and anticipate how God might respond to our prayers. **T**/F

Essay-type Questions

1. Explain the technological rationale of prayer in the Bible.

   [500 words or less]

2. Identify one of the prayer apps. Explain the reason why you think it is beneficial.

   [250 words or less].

3. Conduct a research on the 12 prayer apps identified in this chapter. What element/s would you wish to recommend for the next generation of prayer app innovations? Cite a Bible verse/s to support your view.

   [1,500 words or less].

Multiple-choice Questions

1. The university of prayer informs two factors:

    A. Glory and favor
    B. Glory and power
    C. Favor and honor
    D. Favor and majesty

2. The "Lord's Prayer" is ___

    A. Both a regulatory and a model prayer
    B. Only a regulatory prayer
    C. Only a model prayer
    D. Neither a regulatory nor a model prayer

3. "Our Father" is a ___ factor in the "Lord's Prayer."

    A. Glory
    B. Favor
    C. Both glory and favor
    D. Neither a glory nor a favor

4. Through the juxtaposition of ___ and ___ we have this rare combination of favor and glory enshrined in one event.

   A. Father and Son
   B. Holiness and Holy Spirit
   C. Father and holiness
   D. Holiness and honor

5. The greatest hindrance to prayer is ___

   A. Lack of faith
   B. Unrepentance
   C. Prayerlessness
   D. Unforgiveness

6. What is the ultimate purpose of prayer, whether prayed individually or in mass, corporate prayer?

   A. Universal order
   B. Happiness
   C. Peace
   D. Unspeakable joy

7. What is one of the central tenets that keeps all of God's children in union with Him till Jesus Christ comes back?

   A. Prayer
   B. Fasting
   C. Temptations
   D. Dancing

8. "Give us this day our daily bread," is a _____ to praying:

   A. Principled-approach
   B. Naïve-approach
   C. New Testament-approach
   D. Divine-approach

True/False Questions

1. The true university of prayer must embrace glory and favor themes.   **T**/F

2. Jesus knew that we would have a troublesome life here on earth because of the presence of evil and the devil.   **T**/F

3. There is no proven way of evading sin and sinfulness other than prayer.   **T**/F

4. "Kingdom come" and "daily bread" are the only glory themes in the Lord's Prayer.
   T/**F**

5. Grace (favor) is an infinite refrain from God's perspective.   T/**F**

6. God doesn't wish that all the people of the world should live as He does. T/**F**

7. Prayer is the most important affair of the day; those who pray daily, also enjoy relatively less stressful and evil dealings.   **T**/F

Essay-type Questions

1. The Explain the security of food in relation to the Lord's Prayer

   [500 words or less].

2. Give a rationale for the university of prayer.

   [500 words or less].

3. Identify at least five (5) benefits of being children of God. Why is it important to belong to the family of God? If children of God, how ought we to pray?

   [500 words or less].

54 | Prayer and Politics

Multiple-choice Questions

1. The national day of prayer policy should:

    A. Be based on politics
    B. Be framed around the whims of government
    C. Be based on a dual and mutual understanding of governmental and religious jurisdictions
    D. Be based on the Bible alone

2. "The acknowledgment of the sovereignty of God over the land and His relationship to His people," is a ____

    A. Content of prayer
    B. An Old Testament deduction
    C. Procedural requirement
    D. Policy statement

3. The Prayer of Jehoshaphat connotes very closely to ____

    A. The historical attack by the Moabites
    B. The national day of prayer
    C. The Lord's Prayer
    D. Proper leadership ethics

4. The classic national prayer advisory has ___ parts.

   A. 2
   B. 4
   C. 3
   D. 5

5. The lynchpin of any nation that desires to thrive in righteousness and prosperity is ___

   A. Prayer
   B. Good leadership
   C. Morality
   D. Good governance

True/False Questions

1. Both the USA and Zambia have national days of prayer.   **T**/F

2. National day of prayers must be creatures of politics alone. T/**F**

3. When a nation gathers to pray, many competing interests are involved.   **T**/F

4. The International Day of Prayer for the Persecuted Church falls on the first Sunday of November.   **T**/F

5. The Old Testament national prayer was a matter of individualized preference.   T/**F**

6. Paul advises that prayer must be made for kings only.   T/**F**

7. The language of the day of prayer must be such that it does not evoke political indoctrinations.   **T**/F

8. In national days of prayer, the audience is God alone.   T/**F**

9. Being under Roman colonial control made it impractical to conduct public prayers in Israel.   **T**/F

10. The content of the prayers offered at national days of prayer must be in tune with the elements that constitute the audience.   **T**/F

Essay-type Questions

1. Justify the Prayer of Jehoshaphat in relation to the Lord's Prayer

   [500 words or less].

2. List and explain the seven points that must be taken into consideration when designating national prayer days .
   [
   500 words or less].

3. "There is a subtle connection between the rebuilding of the wall of Jerusalem and the temple." Explain how politics complement religion.

   [250 words or less].

4. List and describe the principles of national prayer.

   [500 words or less].

5. "National days of prayer necessitates the synergizing of these two ideals – a deserved leadership and an obedient people." Explain

   [250 or less words].

55 | Introduction to the Tabernacle

Multiple-choice Questions

1. Whose idea was the tabernacle?

   A. God's
   B. Man's
   C. Moses'
   D. Aaron's

2. Red is a symbol of ____

   A. Salvation
   B. Perfect man
   C. Divinity
   D. Acacia wood

3. The name of Jesus mostly depictive of the tabernacle is ____

   A. Emmanuel
   B. Savior
   C. Messiah
   D. Christ

4. The High Priest wore a cloak known as ___

   A. Phylactery
   B. Ephod
   C. Gown
   D. Litany

5. In the ___ were twelve stones depicting the twelve tribes of Israel.

   A. Phylactery
   B. Ephod
   C. Gown
   D. Litany

True/False Questions

1. The anointing oil carries the presence of the real Holy Spirit.   T/**F**

2. Acacia wood is also known as shittim wood.
   T/F

3. Intercessors should have mercy but not pity.
   T/**F**

4. Jesse was a Capernaumite.   T/**F**

5. Jesus died as Lion and yet He was a Lamb.
   T/**F**

6. Purple stands for legality.   T/**F**

7. God wants silver and gold from us because He is broke.   T/**F**

8. Biblical symbolism shows us that Mark's Gospel focuses on Christ's purity.
   T/F

9. David was set apart as king over Israel by the anointing.   **T**/F

10. Tabernacle literally means a portable sanctuary.   **T**/F

Essay-type Questions

1. Complete the table below:

Item	What it stands for
Gold	
	Redemption
Brass/bronze	
	Son of God
Purple	
	Salvation
White/linen	
	Prophetic voice
Ram's skin dyed red	
	Unattractiveness
Acacia/shittim wood	
	Fragrance/beauty

56 | Construction of the Tabernacle

Multiple-choice Questions

1. The tabernacle was divided into three parts. Which one does not form that composition?

   A. Outer Court
   B. Holy Place
   C. Holy of Holies
   D. Gate

2. Each of these formed the composition of the Outer Court, except ___

   A. Fence
   B. Gate
   C. Altar of burnt offering
   D. Ark

3. The fence to the Outer Court of the tabernacle was made of ___

   A. Badger skin
   B. Bronze
   C. Silver
   D. Goat skin

4. The other name for the altar of burnt offering was ___

   A. Brazen altar
   B. Burnt incense
   C. Silvery altar
   D. Calvary

5. The boards of the fence of the Outer Court were also known as ___

   A. Poles
   B. Drywallers
   C. Acacia wood
   D. Beams

6. The boards of the fence of the Outer Court were made from ___

   A. Hard acacia wood
   B. Incorruptible acacia wood
   C. Cut, cleaned and clothed acacia wood
   D. All of the above are correct

7. The gate to the Outer Court had ___ colors.

   A. 2
   B. 3
   C. 4
   D. 5

8. All these colors were in the gate to the Outer Court of the tabernacle, except ____

   A. Blue
   B. Purple
   C. Scarlet
   D. Grey

9. In appearance, all these apply to a badger, except ____

   A. Dull
   B. Ugly
   C. Beautiful
   D. Grey

10. "It was for Aaron and his sons to wash their hands and feet in as they served in the tabernacle." What was it?

    A. Laver
    B. Altar
    C. Basin
    D. Folks

True/False Questions

1. The laver was made of bronze.   **T**/F

2. If Aaron or his children did not wash at laver they might die.   T/**F**

3. The laver stood between the altar of burnt offering and the door of the sanctuary.
   T/F

4. The sanctuary consisted of the Holy Place and Holy of Holies.   **T**/F

5. There are details given concerning the size of the laver.   T/**F**

Essay-type Questions

1. List and describe the characteristics of the laver.

    [500 words or less].

2. Relate the laver to a life of prayer using scriptural references.

    [500 or less words].

3. List and describe the characteristics of the altar of burnt offering.

    [500 words or less].

4. Relate the altar of burnt offering to a life of prayer using scriptural references.

    [500 or less words].

5. List and describe the characteristics of the gate.

    [500 words or less].

6. Relate the gate to a life of prayer using scriptural references.

    [500 or less words].

57 | The Outer Court

Multiple-choice Questions

1. How many times did the High Priest enter into the Holy of Holies?

   A. Once every year
   B. Twice every year
   C. Three times every
   D. Never

2. Coriander seeds are generally believed to represent ___

   A. Resurrection
   B. Fragrance
   C. Sweetness
   D. Preciousness

3. The mercy seat was made of ___

   A. Gold
   B. Silver
   C. Bronze
   D. Bdellium

4. The instructions to construct the tabernacle was from ____

    A. Inside out
    B. Throne to the gate
    C. Divinity to humanity
    D. All of the above

5. The sanctuary was divided in two by a ____

    A. Veil
    B. Cherubim
    C. Aaron's curtain
    D. Hedge of fire

6. All these constituted the contents of the Ark, except ____

    A. Law
    B. Rod
    C. Manna
    D. Almonds

7. The ultimate end of the tabernacle was ____

    A. Prayer
    B. Worship
    C. Glory
    D. Fear of God

8. The current status whereby believers in Christ can represent people before God and at the same time represent God before the people, is called ___

    A. Regal
    B. Legal
    C. Royal priesthood
    D. Holy nation

9. The relationship among the contents of the ark is that ___

    A. One is food, a tree and a law
    B. One is earthly and two are divine
    C. They all came from God
    D. They can be lost easily

10. The glory that sat on the Mercy Seat is sometimes known as ___

    A. Effordance glory
    B. Effulgence glory
    C. Shekinah glory
    D. Barrack

True/False Questions

1. High Priest Aaron entered into the Holy of Holies with the blood of animals.   **T**/F

2. It was uncertain whether Aaron would return dead or alive when he entered into the Holy of Holies.
   T/F

3. Christ was perfect, knew no sin and was made sin for us. **T**/F

4. The blood of Abel, bulls and goats could permanently take away the sins of the people. T/**F**

5. Because of Christ's death on Calvary, God has accepted us in and has called us His children.
   T/F

6. Exactly 50,700 men of Bethlehem one day died for trying to remove the lid and peep into the Ark.
   T/**F**

7. Gospel means Gossip News.   T/**F**

8. The Ark found its final resting place in the temple that Solomon built.   **T**/F

9. When power meets mercy, the result is grace.
   T/F

10. The priesthood of Jesus Christ is patterned upon Aaron's.   T/**F**

Essay-type Questions

1. Design the sanctuary from the description given in this chapter.

   a) What are its component features?
   b) What is the general purpose of the sanctuary?
   c) Why do you think the sanctuary was square in shape?
   d) What qualities make manna a true divine food?
   e) What happened to Aaron's stick?
   f) Which kind of law was included into the ark?
   g) Why is the ark called "Ark of Covenant" or "Ark of Testimony"?
   h) What overshadows the mercy seat and why?
   i) Why is the mercy seat made of gold?
   j) Explain why the structure, contents, purpose of the sanctuary all pointed to Christ.

   [2000 words or less].

58 | The Holy Place

Multiple-choice Questions

1. A table, generally, alludes to all these, except ____

   A. Food
   B. Fellowship
   C. Friendship
   D. Sorrow

2. How many loaves of bread were placed on the table of showbread with frankincense to prepare it for a week before it could be replaced and eaten in the presence of God by the sons of Aaron?

   A. 12
   B. 6
   C. 3
   D. 24

3. In the Holy Place, bread was eaten ____

   A. When fresh
   B. In the presence of God
   C. After seven days
   D. Only by Aaron

4. The Bread of Life gives all these, except ____

    A. Satisfaction
    B. Goodness
    C. Fulfilment
    D. Hunger

5. The knobs on the golden lampstand represented ____

    A. Pomegranates and flowers
    B. Lilies and flowers
    C. Pomegranates and lilies
    D. Flowers and goblets

True/False Questions

1. The showbread table was made of acacia wood.
   T/**F**

2. In the Holy Place, there was perpetual light.
   T/F

3. The purpose of frankincense was to preserve the bread for at least a week.   **T**/F

4. The golden candlelight also symbolized life.
   T/F

5. The candlelight, like the laver, had measurements.
   T/**F**

6. The candlelight had wood in it.   T/**F**

7. The altar of incense was rectangular.   T/**F**

8. The altar of incense, the altar of burnt offering, the laver and the mercy seat were placed in the same line.   **T**/F

9. In God's presence is fullness of joy.   **T**/F

10. At God's right hand is the pleasures called Jesus Christ.   **T**/F

Essay-type Questions

1. Compare the altar of burnt offering in the Outer Court to the altar of incense in the Holy Place of the tabernacle. What the similarities and difference can you identify?

   [250 words or less].

2. Discuss the presence of the showbread in the Holy Place and the fact that Jesus Christ claimed to be the Bread of Life.

   [500 words or less].

3. By using symbolism leaned in Chapter 55, discuss the following: "At the gate, there were four pillars of wood which were overlaid with bronze, while at the door there were five pillars and they were overlaid with gold."

   [500 words or less].

59 | Holy of Holies

Multiple-choice Questions

1. The How many times did the High Priest enter into the Holy of Holies?

    A. Once every year
    B. Twice every year
    C. Three times every
    D. Never

2. Coriander seeds are, generally, believed to represent ___

    A. Resurrection
    B. Fragrance
    C. Sweetness
    D. Preciousness

3. The mercy seat was made of ___

    A. Gold
    B. Silver
    C. Bronze
    D. Bdellium

4. The instructions to construct the tabernacle was from ____

   A. Inside out
   B. Throne to the gate
   C. Divinity to humanity
   D. All of the above

5. The sanctuary was divided in two by a ____

   A. Veil
   B. Cherubim
   C. Aaron's curtain
   D. Hedge of fire

6. All these constituted the contents of the Ark, except ____

   A. Law
   B. Rod
   C. Manna
   D. Almonds

7. The ultimate end of the tabernacle was ____

   E. Prayer
   F. Worship
   G. Glory
   H. Fear of God

8. The current status whereby believers in Christ can represent people before God and at the same time represent God before the people, is called ____

   E. Regal
   F. Legal
   G. Royal priesthood
   A. Holy nation

9. The relationship among the contents of the Ark is that ____

   A. One is food, a tree and a law
   B. One is earthly and two are divine
   C. They all came from God
   D. They can be lost easily

10. The glory that sat on the Mercy Seat is sometimes known as ____

    A. Effordance glory
    B. Effulgence glory
    C. Shekinah glory
    D. Barrack

True/False Questions

1. The High Priest Aaron entered into the Holy of Holies with the blood of animals. **T**/F

2. It was uncertain whether Aaron would return dead or alive when he entered into the Holy of Holies. **T**/F

3. Christ was perfect, knew no sin and was made sin for us. **T**/F

4. The blood of Abel, bulls and goats could permanently take away the sins of the people. T/**F**

5. Because of Christ's death on Calvary, God has accepted us in and has called us His children. **T**/F

6. Exactly 50,700 men of Bethlehem one day died for trying to remove the lid and peep into the Ark. T/**F**

7. Gospel means Gossip News. T/**F**

8. The Ark found its final resting place in the temple that Solomon built. **T**/F

9. When power meets mercy, the result is grace. **T**/F

10. The priesthood of Jesus Christ is patterned upon Aaron's. T/**F**

Essay-type Questions

1. The Design the sanctuary from the description given in this chapter.

a) What are its component features?
b) What is the general purpose of the sanctuary?
c) Why was the sanctuary square in shape?
d) What qualities make manna a true divine food?
e) What happened to Aaron's stick?
f) Which kind of law was put into the Ark?
g) Why is the Ark called "Ark of Covenant" or "Ark of Testimony"?
h) What overshadowed the mercy seat and why?
i) Why was the mercy seat made of gold?
j) State the reason why the structure, contents, and purpose of the sanctuary all pointed to Christ.

[2000 words or less].

2. List and briefly discuss at least five representations of manna.

[250 words or less].

60 | Benefits of God's Presence

Multiple-choice Questions

1. God's presence must be ___

   A. Everything
   B. Everywhere
   C. Coveted
   D. All of the above

2. Each of these sought the presence of God, except ___

   A. Satan
   B. Moses
   C. David
   D. All of them sought God's presence without exception

3. Each of these words is related to the benefits of the presence of God except ___

   A. Confidence
   B. Failure
   C. Victory
   D. Blessings

4. What is to the fullness in the presence of God?

   A. Character formation
   B. Joy
   C. Anointing
   D. All of the above

5. Which of God's names conceptualizes His presence?

   A. I AM
   B. Jireh
   C. Rapha
   D. Jehovah

True/False Questions

1. God's presence brings victory.   **T**/F

2. When you are with God, you cannot fail.
   T/F

3. God's presence is intimidating.   T/**F**

4. Those who did mightily also loved to be in the presence of God, for example, Moses and David.   **T**/F

5. Confidence is not one of the benefits of the presence of God.   T/**F**

6. In biblical parlance, favor and grace are the same things. T/**F**

7. Seeking first the Kingdom of God and His righteousness is the same as seeking the presence of God. **T**/F

8. It is better to seek the blesser than the blessing, because the blessing will always be with the blesser. **T**/F

9. Even Satan has sought God's presence before. **T**/F

10. Prayer is the foremost and quintessential mode of seeking God's presence. **T**/F

Essay-type Questions

1. In relation to the presence of God, discuss how the hare (deer)'s character and strategy fits in very well within some of the benefits of the presence of God.

   [2000 words or less].

About the Author

Charles Mwewa (LLB. BA. Edu. + Engl., BA. Legal Studies. Cert. Law. DIBM. LLM.) is a Dad, author, lawyer, licensed paralegal, educator, moral, spiritual and social influencer, and leader. Mwewa is the author of over 50 books and counting in all genres – fiction (novels), non-fiction and poetry. Mwewa, his wife, and their three girls, reside in the Capital City of Ottawa, Canada

Websites:
charlesmwewa.com
acpress.ca

Facebook:
https://www.facebook.com/profile.php?id=100086693478517

Email:
info@acpress.ca

Amazon
https://www.amazon.ca/dp/1988251117
https://www.amazon.ca/dp/1998788180

Scriptural References Used in the Main Text

1 Kings 17:20-21
1 Kings 18:27-29
1 Kings 18:36
1 Kings 18:38
1 Kings 18:41-19:8
1 Kings 18:41-44
1 Kings 18:42
1 Kings 19:1, 18
1 Kings 19:11-13
1 Kings 19:16
1 Kings 19:9-11
1 Kings 2:18-20
1 Kings 21:27
1 Kings 3:4
1 Kings 3:5ff
1 Kings 6
1 Kings 8:22
1 Kings 8:22-53
1 Kings 8:22-61
1 Kings 8:46
1 Kings 8:54
1 Kings 8:63
1 Peter 1:15-17
1 Peter 1:17
1 Peter 1:19
1 Peter 1:4
1 Peter 2:22
1 Peter 2:24
1 Peter 2:5
1 Peter 2:7
1 Peter 2:9
1 Peter 3:10-11
1 Peter 3:18
1 Peter 3:9
1 Peter 4:8
1 Peter 5:6
1 Peter 5:6-9

1 Peter 5:7
1 Peter 5:8
1 Peter 5:8-9
1 Samuel 1:9-10
1 Samuel 16:13
1 Samuel 16:1-3
1 Samuel 23:3, 4
1 Sam 24:12-15
1 Samuel 7:5-9, 12:23
and 15:11
1 Samuel 1:11-13
1 Samuel 1:26
1 Samuel 10:1
1 Samuel 10:6
1 Samuel 10:9
1 Samuel 12:23
1 Samuel 15:18
1 Samuel 16:13
1 Samuel 16:14-18
1 Samuel 16:7
1 Samuel 18:17
1 Samuel 2:35
1 Samuel 25:22
1 Samuel 26:23
1 Samuel 4:21
1 Samuel 6:12
1 Samuel 6:19
1 Samuel 7: 6
1 Samuel 7:5
1 Samuel 9:13
1 Samuel 10:1
1 Samuel 10:6
1 Samuel 10:7
1 Thessalonians 3:5
1 Thessalonians 5:17–19
1 Thessalonians 5:18
1 Thessalonians 5:19

Acts 6:1-7
Acts 6:6, 13:3
Acts 7:60
Acts 8:14-17, 19:6
Acts 8:17
Acts 8:22
Acts 9:10
Acts 9:9
Amos 1:2
Amos 3:3
Amos 3:7
Amos 4:5
Amos 7:2, 3, 5-6
Colossians 2:7
Colossians 1:16
Colossians 2:14
Colossians 4:12
Colossians 4:19
Colossians 4:9
Colossians 3:12-14
Colossians 3:15
Colossians 3:15
Colossians 3:5
Colossians 4:12
Daniel 10: 2-3
Daniel 10:12-13
Daniel 10:13, 20
Daniel 10:21
Daniel 10:3
Daniel 10:3-12
Daniel 10:6
Daniel 10:9-11
Daniel 12:1
Daniel 12:4
Daniel 2:1 - 13
Daniel 6
Daniel 6:10

Daniel 6:22
Daniel 8:16 and 9:21
Deuteronomy 21:22
Deuteronomy 26: 13 and 14
Deuteronomy 26:15
Deuteronomy 28:1-2
Deuteronomy 28:15
Deuteronomy 30:11
Deuteronomy 32:30
Deuteronomy 33:6-11
Deuteronomy 5:9
Deuteronomy 6:16
Deuteronomy 6:4
Deuteronomy 6:4-25
Deuteronomy 8:18
Deuteronomy 8:2
Deuteronomy 8:3
Ecclesiastes 3:21
Ecclesiastes 5:2-3
Ecclesiastes 7:20
Ecclesiastes 9:11
Ephesians 1:10
Ephesians 1:11
Ephesians 1:13
Ephesians 1:20-21; 6:12
Ephesians 1:20-22
Ephesians 1:21
Ephesians 1:3
Ephesians 1:4-5
Ephesians 1:5
Ephesians 2:14-16
Ephesians 2:1-8
Ephesians 2:4-5
Ephesians 2:5-6
Ephesians 2:8
Ephesians 2:8-9

Hebrews 9:22

Hebrews 9:22

Hosea 10:12

Hosea 4:6

Hosea 4:6-7

1 Corinthians 15:57

I Peter 5:7

Isaiah 1:15

Isaiah 10:27

Isaiah 14:11-13

Isaiah 14:12

Isaiah 14:12-15

Isaiah 14:13-14

Isaiah 2:2-3

Isaiah 30:19

Isaiah 33:16

Isaiah 33:2

Isaiah 33:22

Isaiah 4:1

Isaiah 40:22

Isaiah 40:31

Isaiah 40:31

Isaiah 41:10

Isaiah 41:4

Isaiah 42:1

Isaiah 42:13

Isaiah 42:13-17

Isaiah 42:8

Isaiah 42:8

Isaiah 43:19

Isaiah 43:27

Isaiah 45:11

Isaiah 45:23

Isaiah 47:10

Isaiah 48:6

Isaiah 49:9

Isaiah 5:20

Isaiah 5:20

Isaiah 53:26

Isaiah 54:10

Isaiah 54:17

Isaiah 55: 1

Isaiah 55:11

Isaiah 55:4

Isaiah 55:6

Isaiah 55:7

Isaiah 55:8-9

Isaiah 56:7

Isaiah 58:11

Isaiah 58:13

Isaiah 58:14

Isaiah 58:6-14

Isaiah 58:8

Isaiah 59:12-16

Isaiah 59:16

Isaiah 6:3

Isaiah 60:22.

Isaiah 61:1

Isaiah 61:3

Isaiah 62: 6-7

Isaiah 62:6-7

Isaiah 62:7

Isaiah 64:1

Isaiah 64:6

Isaiah 66:1

Isaiah 66:7-9

James 1:22-23

James 1:6

James 2:17

James 2:19

James 2:23

James 3:1

James 4:14

James 4:2

Leviticus 20:10
Leviticus 23:26-32
Leviticus 24 5-10
Leviticus 24:1-4
Leviticus 8:30
Leviticus 8:30
Luke 1:11
Luke 1:26
Luke 1:28
Luke 1:50
Luke 1:55,72
Luke 10:19
Luke 10:41-42
Luke 11:1
Luke 11:11-13
Luke 11:13
Luke 11:2
Luke 11:5-13
Luke 11:5-8
Luke 12:22-26
Luke 12:32
Luke 12:32
Luke 12:7
Luke 15:10
Luke 15:11-32
Luke 15:3–7
Luke 16:22
Luke 16:23
Luke 16:23-24
Luke 17:15
Luke 17:20-29
Luke 17:6
Luke 18:1
Luke 18:1-8
Luke 18:18-13
Luke 18:30
Luke 18:9-14

Luke 2:14
Luke 2:19
Luke 2:37
Luke 20:34-36
Luke 21:11b
Luke 22:20
Luke 22:29-46
Luke 22:32
Luke 22:41
Luke 23:32
Luke 23:34
Luke 23:43
Luke 23:46
Luke 23:46
Luke 24:50
Luke 24:52-53
Luke 3:16
Luke 3:16
Luke 3:22
Luke 4: 18-19
Luke 4:14
Luke 4:4, 8, 12
Luke 4:5-6
Luke 5:17
Luke 6:12, 13
Luke 6:13
Luke 6:27-28
Luke 6:28-29
Luke 6:37
Luke 6:38
Luke 6:45
Luke 8:16
Luke 8:29
Luke 9:16
Luke 9:28-43
Luke 9:29
Luke. 23:34

Luke. 4:1
Luke23:38
Malachi 2:1-2
Malachi 3:16
Malachi 3:6
Malachi 3:7–12
Mark 1:15
Mark 1:26ff
Mark 1:4
Mark 10:30
Mark 11:12-25
Mark 11:2
Mark 11:22
Mark 11:22-25
Mark 11:23
Mark 11:23-24
Mark 11:23-24
Mark 11:23-24
Mark 11:24
Mark 11:25
Mark 13:37
Mark 14:25
Mark 14:38
Mark 14:8
Mark 15:34
Mark 16:15-18
Mark 16:17
Mark 5: 1-20
Mark 5:11-13
Mark 5:1-20
Mark 5:2-11
Mark 5:22-24
Mark 5:3
Mark 5:6-13
Mark 6:46
Mark 7:34
Mark 8:34-38

Mark 9:23
Mark 9:29
Mark 9:34-44
Mark 9:43
Mark 9:43-44
Matthew 18:19-20
Mathew 27:46
Matthew 4:1-11
Matthew 6:16
Mathew 6:17
Matthew 6:6
Matthew 6:7
Matthew 27:46
Matthew 1:20
Matthew 1:22-23
Matthew 10:16-20
Matthew 10:28
Matthew 10:8
Matthew 11: 28-30
Matthew 11:12
Matthew 11:12
Matthew 11:25
Matthew 11:28
Matthew 11:5
Matthew 12:24
Matthew 12:31
Matthew 12:32
Matthew 12:34-35
Matthew 12:36-37
Matthew 12:43-45
Matthew 12:45
Matthew 13:42
Matthew 14:23
Matthew 15:14
Matthew 15:19
Matthew 15:36
Matthew 15:8

Proverbs 28:25
Proverbs 3:33
Proverbs 3:9
Proverbs 30:7-9
Proverbs 30:8
Proverbs 31:8-9
Proverbs 4:23
Proverbs 8:10-11
Proverbs 8:13
Psalm 10:5
Psalm 10:6
Psalm 100:4
Psalm 100:4
Psalm 103:12
Psalm 104:5-6
Psalm 11:1
Psalm 116:17
Psalm 119:21
Psalm 119:48
Psalm 121
Psalm 122:6
Psalm 125:2
Psalm 126:1-3
Psalm 126:5-6
Psalm 127:1
Psalm 133:2
Psalm 134:2
Psalm 139:2
Psalm 139:3-4
Psalm 139:4
Psalm 139:7-10
Psalm 141:2
Psalm 147:1
Psalm 147:1
Psalm 148.2
Psalm 148.5
Psalm 149:6-8

Psalm 150:1b
Psalm 150:6
Psalm 16:10
Psalm 16:11
Psalm 18:1
Psalm 18:2-4
Psalm 18:4-5
Psalm 18:7
Psalm 19:1
Psalm 19:14
Psalm 2:8
Psalm 22
Psalm 22
Psalm 22:3
Psalm 23:5
Psalm 24:1
Psalm 24:1-2
Psalm 24:4
Psalm 25:18
Psalm 26:2
Psalm 27:1
Psalm 27:13
Psalm 28:2
Psalm 28:7
Psalm 29:10
Psalm 29:3,10
Psalm 3:5
Psalm 30:5
Psalm 31:15
Psalm 32:8
Psalm 33:8
Psalm 34:7
Psalm 34:8
Psalm 35:13
Psalm 35:5-6
Psalm 39:12
Psalm 4:1

Psalm 4:8

Psalm 42:1-2

Psalm 42:6

Psalm 44:21

Psalm 45:7

Psalm 45:8

Psalm 46:1

Psalm 5:3

Psalm 50:14

Psalm 50:15

Psalm 50:23

Psalm 51:17

Psalm 51:5b

Psalm 52:7

Psalm 55:17

Psalm 6:9

Psalm 61:1

Psalm 61:2

Psalm 62:10

Psalm 63:1-2

Psalm 63:4

Psalm 68:1

Psalm 69:10

Psalm 7:11

Psalm 7:9

Psalm 73:12

Psalm 73:28

Psalm 77:2

Psalm 8:2

Psalm 8:3-8

Psalm 8:4

Psalm 84:10

Psalm 84:1-2

Psalm 84:3-4

Psalm 91:1

Psalm 91:11

Psalm 91:11-16

Psalm 91:15

Psalm 91:2,4,5,7,9 and 11

Psalm 91:9-14

Psalm 94:19

Psalm 95: 1-2

Psalm 95:6

Psalm 96:46

Psalm 96:9

Psalm 97

Psalm 106:6

Psalm 119:66

Psalm 148:1-14

Psalm 89:14

Psalm 9:17

Revelation 1:13, 7:17

Revelation 1:17

Revelation 1:6

Revelation 10:3

Revelation 12:1; 18:1

Revelation 12:10

Revelation 12:11

Revelation 12:12

Revelation 12:16-19

Revelation 12:4

Revelation 12:7

Revelation 12:7-13; 20:2

Revelation 12:7-9

Revelation 12:9

Revelation 12:9

Revelation 12:9,12, 20:2

Revelation 12:9; 20:2

Revelation 14:10; 16:19:15

Revelation 14:13

Revelation 17:1-6

Revelation 19:20

Revelation 19:20

Zechariah 1:9 13-14, 19
Zechariah 10:1
Zechariah 12:10
Zechariah 3:1

Zechariah 3:1-10
Zechariah 3:2
Zechariah 4:7

Sources Cited in the Main Text

Holy Bible

"Belligerent," < https://guide-humanitarian-law.org/content/article/3/belligerent/>

"Earthquakes: Seismographs & Technology," https://schoolworkhelper.net/earthquakes-seismographs-technology/#

"Enemy alien," < https://www.collinsdictionary.com/dictionary/english/enemy-alien>

"Names of Satan," < https://www.uua.org/re/tapestry/youth/bridges/workshop16/names-satan>

"Right" from https://languages.oup.com/google-dictionary-en/?

"Tabernacle," https://www.britannica.com/topic/Tabernacle

"The Jewish Temples: The First Temple - Solomon's Temple," https://www.jewishvirtuallibrary.org/the-first-temple-solomon-s-temple

3 6 U.S.C. § 119: US Code – Section 119: National Day of Prayer

Al Early, "Is 'forgive and forget' Biblical?" *The Winchester Sun*, July 28th, 2017

Bible Gateway, "Dictionary of bible themes – 5467 promises, divine," < https://www.biblegateway.com/resources/dictionary -of-bible-themes/5467-promises-divine>

Bibleinfo, "How many Bible promises are there?," < https://www.bibleinfo.com/en/questions/how-many-bible-promises-are-there>

Bob Edgar, General Secretary of the National Council of Churches

Britannica, "Ark of the Covenant," https://www.britannica.com/topic/Ark-of-the-Covenant

CBC News, "Microchip implants in humans on the market," November 2002

Charles Mwewa, *Resurrection (A Spy in Hell)* (Ottawa: ACP, 2022)

Charles Mwewa, *The Patch Theorem: A philosophy of death, life and time* (Ottawa: ACP, 2022)

Chasing Vibrance, "Promises of God in the Bible to Claim Everyday," October 27th, 2020 < https://chasingvibrance.com/promises-of-god-in-the-bible-to-claim-everyday/>

CTV News, "New technology could turn Smartphone into virtual wallet," July 6th, 2011

Dictionary.law.com, "Right."

Graham-Suit v. Clainos, 756 F.3d 724, 749-50 (9th Cir. 2013)

HD Livingstone, "Jewish Burial Customs and Anointing Oils," October 10, 2017 < https://classroom.synonym.com/jewish-burial-customs-and-anointing-oils-12087702.html>

https://3dwarehouse.sketchup.com/model/5308991be9bd083fad8a06dbee1d115/Herods-Temple

https://get.tithe.ly/blog/technology-in-the-bible

https://www.jewishvirtuallibrary.org/the-first-temple-solomon-s-temple)

https://www.progress-index.com/story/lifestyle/faith/2009/11/28/pastor-explains-significance-veil-being/985994007/

https://www.theGospelcoalition.org/blogs/justin-taylor/what-does-the-tabernacle-symbolize/

Lord Alfred Tennyson, 1809-92

MasterClass, "Writing 101: What Is Chiasmus? Learn About the Rhetorical Device with Examples," < https://www.masterclass.com/articles/writing-101-what-is-chiasmus-learn-about-the-rhetorical-device-with-examples>

Merriam-Webster Dictionary, "Covenant," <
https://www.merriam-
webster.com/dictionary/covenant#:~:text=%3A%20
a%20written%20agreement%20or%20promise,coven
antal>

Merriam-Webster, "Essential Meaning of promise," <
https://www.merriam-
webster.com/dictionary/promise>

O. Palmer Robertson, *The Christ of the Covenants*
(Phillipsburg: P&R Publishing, 1980)

Presidential Statutory Instrument No.78 of 2015, and
Gazette Notice of October 23rd, 2015

Richard II, 1595

Samuel Taylor Coleridge, 1772-1834

Theology of Work Project, "Rebuilding the Wall of
Jerusalem (Nehemiah 1:1-7:73),"
https://www.theologyofwork.org/old-
testament/ezra-nehemiah-
esther/nehemiah/restoration-of-the-wall-of-
jerusalem-nehemiah-11-773

Word International Ministries, Ontario